How Autism Is Reshaping
Special Education

How Autism Is Reshaping Special Education

The Unbundling of IDEA

Mark K. Claypool and John M. McLaughlin

ROWMAN & LITTLEFIELD
Lanham • Boulder • New York • London

KH

Published by Rowman & Littlefield
A wholly owned subsidiary of The Rowman & Littlefield Publishing Group, Inc.
4501 Forbes Boulevard, Suite 200, Lanham, Maryland 20706
www.rowman.com

Unit A, Whitacre Mews, 26-34 Stannary Street, London SE11 4AB

British Library Cataloguing in Publication Information Available

Library of Congress Cataloging-in-Publication Data

ISBN 978-1-4758-3496-3 (cloth : alk. paper)
ISBN 978-1-4758-3497-0 (pbk. : alk. paper)
ISBN 978-1-4758-3498-7 (electronic)

∞ ™ The paper used in this publication meets the minimum requirements of American National Standard for Information Sciences Permanence of Paper for Printed Library Materials, ANSI/NISO Z39.48-1992.

Printed in the United States of America

9/15/17

To parents, teachers, and therapists at the intersection of autism and special education.

Contents

Foreword

When my son, Winston, was diagnosed with autism in 2003, his prognosis was bleak—hopeless, heartbreaking, devastating. I had two other children and another on the way. My husband was in medical school, and the very last thing we expected to hear from the developmental pediatrician was the suggestion that we apply for Medicaid as soon as possible. We were told that our son would most likely never be a contributing member of society and to expect institutionalization by age 13. Several weeks and buckets of midnight tears later, with the help of family and friends, I got my wits about me and found Ann Eldridge and Early Autism Project in Sumter, South Carolina.

Winston was enrolled in a church preschool program at the time. I showed up unannounced one day and watched as the class prepared for pick-up time. The children put away their belongings and then went to sit in a circle. After everyone was sitting "crisscross applesauce," they went to the cubby wall, put on their coats, got their backpacks, and waited in a straight line. But Winston never moved from his spot on the carpet. He was playing with the dust particles dancing around in the sunlight streaming through the window.

As his classmates filed out of the room to meet their parents, the teacher approached Winston and encouraged him to come get ready for me. He needed her undivided attention; he was unable to do anything by himself. We withdrew him from the program the following day. I could not think much beyond the end of the week, but Ann did. She trained our therapists and developed a plan of attack unlike no other. Within the first two weeks of applied behavior analysis, my child, who had never uttered anything but a blood-curdling scream, was signing for "milk," "more," "swing," and, of course, "cookie."

After reenrolling, Winston was able to work, learn, and grow in a structured church school program. Our Board Certified Behavior Analyst had access to him during school hours and was able to see firsthand where he was struggling and to make programming adjustments to address areas of deficit. The result was nothing short of a miracle. His hard work and determination, coupled with her skill and expertise and the commitment of his line therapists, was a perfect trifecta. Winston was off to public school in the fall.

Public school was not an easy transition. While we had a wonderful teacher, after the first couple of months, we realized how critical Winston's shadow was going to be in determining educational success (or failure). She was my eyes and ears in school, but she did not understand him, us, or what the district autism itinerant was asking of her, so I asked for another shadow. I begged and pleaded. I explained in painstaking detail what he needed and what we wanted. My words fell mostly on deaf ears.

I began working to pass legislation to mandate equity for autism treatment in South Carolina. Our grassroots mission spread quickly. We called friends and asked them to call friends, and they called their friends, and so on. That was our tactic. It created a local stir that drew attention to Winston and his situation. I think the director of special education heard me, but her hands were tied; lack of funding prevented her from hiring another shadow or from training the shadows who were already employed by the district. Our district was considered by many to be "autism friendly." And yet, there we were due to lack of funding.

When my colleague, Lorri Unumb, asked me to join her efforts to seek insurance parity for autism treatment, I had no idea what I was getting myself into. I don't think either one of us did. Along with another mother of a child with autism, we worked day and night, organizing, writing, calling, emailing, researching, and praying. And despite our best efforts, we failed. We lost. It was crushing, and it was personal. But there was a silver lining. We were able to establish a public health program through our Department of Disabilities and Special Needs, a Medicaid waiver, which allowed us to enroll upwards of 100 children in a treatment program that mirrored what we were asking the insurance companies to cover.

And while that was not our original mission, the prospect of creating a public health program that would allow 60 percent of children in our state to have a chance at treatment—the same treatment my husband and I had been paying thousands of dollars for privately—made it clear to me that our legislators were almost believers, but they needed proof that it worked. They wanted to do the right thing, and the majority cared. We also knew they cared about their constituents. We met with almost every single legislator. And the legislators met with their constituents—parents and extended families who took time away from their jobs and commitments to seek out their state senators and house members and ask for help.

As I traveled across the state and met with families to garner support for our insurance bill, I realized how complete hopelessness and helplessness embraced many of them. These families had limited support and woefully inadequate educational opportunities, and treatment choices were few and far between. In response, my husband and I decided to establish Winston's Wish Foundation, a nonprofit dedicated to improving the lives of children with autism and their families in South Carolina.

How Autism Is Reshaping Special Education: The Unbundling of IDEA is a must-read for parents, educators, and professionals who are seeking an informative and accurate barometer on the current climate of special education, the potential blending of medical and educational models, and the pros and cons of policy. The book also provides an excellent crash course in the history and potential outlook for the IDEA and represents both sides of this story.

Like the other advocates and parents interviewed for the book, I will not apologize for advocating for increased funding for autism treatment, education, improved outcomes, and insurance parity. It is shameful to pit parents of children with special needs against one another. Creativity, connectivity, and a willingness to listen and seek compromise go a long way in finding solutions and exceeding expectations.

As I read this book, I realized the authors and I have a shared dedication to education, to understanding conflict, and to resolving problems without compromising our steadfast belief in what we know to be the most effective road for our children, a road which is best described by Sherzod Abdukadirov as one in which schools are measured by what they accomplish rather than by what they do.

I agree with the authors' conclusion that, with the unbundling of the IDEA, hope will abound once again—hope for a brighter tomorrow, for dreams fulfilled, and independence gained. I have seen firsthand what collaboration and compromise in public schools and politics can accomplish. Our insurance bill ultimately passed in 2007, but not without a tremendous amount of effort on the part of families across South Carolina, the advocates, and the lawmakers who led the way.

Winston is now a freshman in high school and thrives in a general education placement with full shadow support. He is unaware of the daily struggles his team and I face with the school administration and faculty. But we march on because we are not seeking a minimally adequate educational opportunity. I do not expect the school to "cure" his autism. I do, however, expect the school to provide him with the very best education possible.

Marcella Ridley
November 2016

Preface

Forty Years after the Implementation of the Education for All Handicapped Children Act 1977–2017

I am certainly not an advocate for frequent and untried changes in laws and constitutions. I think moderate imperfections had better be borne with; because, when once known, we accommodate ourselves to them, and find practical means of correcting their ill effects. But I know also, that laws and institutions must go hand in hand with the progress of the human mind. As that becomes more developed, more enlightened, as new discoveries are made, new truths disclosed, and manners and opinions change with the change of circumstances, institutions must advance also, and keep pace with the times. We might as well require a man to wear still the coat which fitted him when a boy, as civilized society to remain ever under the regimen of their barbarous ancestors.

—Thomas Jefferson to H. Tompkinson (aka Samuel Kercheval)
July 12, 1816, 40 years after writing the Declaration of Independence

Acknowledgments

The authors wish to thank the professionals who offer their perspectives in this book. We greatly appreciate their participation in the interview process and in the editing process to assure the accuracy of their thoughts and words. In addition, the authors thank Katarzyna Scherr, our research and editorial associate, not only for managing the interview and editing schedule, but also for her research in identifying many of the individuals interviewed for the book.

Acronyms

AASA	American Association of School Administrators
ABA	Applied Behavior Analysis
ABAI	Association for Behavior Analysis International
ABLE Act	Achieving a Better Life Experience Act
ADA	Americans with Disabilities Act
ADHD	Attention-Deficit/Hyperactivity Disorder
APBA	Association of Professional Behavior Analysts
ASAT	Association for Science in Autism Treatment
ASD	Autism Spectrum Disorder
ASHA	American Speech-Language-Hearing Association
BACB®	Behavior Analyst Certification Board®
BCaBA®	Board Certified Assistant Behavior Analyst®
BCBA®	Board Certified Behavior Analyst®
BEH	Bureau for the Education of the Handicapped
CASE	Council of Administrators of Special Education
CCC-SLP	Certificate of Clinical Competence in Speech-Language Pathology
CDC	Centers for Disease Control and Prevention
CEU	Continuing Education Unit

CMS	Centers for Medicare and Medicaid Services
CP	Cerebral Palsy
CPT	Current Procedural Terminology
DIR	Developmental, Individual Differences, and Relationship-Based Model
DSM-5	*Diagnostic and Statistical Manual of Mental Disorders*
EBD	Emotional and Behavioral Disorder
EHA	Education of the Handicapped Act
EPA	United States Environmental Protection Agency
ESEA	Elementary and Secondary Education Act
ESSA	Every Student Succeeds Act
FAPE	Free Appropriate Public Education
FBA	Functional Behavioral Assessment
FDA	United States Food and Drug Administration
FERPA	Family Educational Rights and Privacy Act
FOIA	Freedom of Information Act
HIPAA	Health Insurance Portability and Accountability Act
ICDL	Interdisciplinary Council on Developmental and Learning Disorders
IDEA	Individuals with Disabilities Education Act
IEP	Individualized Education Program
LD	Learning Disability
LEND	Leadership Education in Neurodevelopmental and Related Disabilities
NCCA	National Commission for Certifying Agencies
NCES	National Center for Education Statistics
NCLB	No Child Left Behind
NIMH	National Institute of Mental Health
OHI	Other Health Impairment

OSEP	Office of Special Education Programs
OT	Occupational Therapy
PBS	Positive Behavior Supports
PDD	Pervasive Developmental Disorder
PT	Physical Therapy
RDA	Results-Driven Accountability
RTI	Response to Intervention
SLP	Speech-Language Pathologist
TCASE	Texas Council of Administrators of Special Education
UDL	Universal Design for Learning

Introduction

Examining the topic of special education and autism touches many sensitive nerves. In conducting research for this book, it was challenging to have some people, in excellent positions to comment on the subject, agree to participate due to concern that this would be another book that treated special education and special educators harshly. We hope that this book has not done that. At the same time, a constant examination of special education or any other aspect of American public education must go on and must be welcomed by the practitioners.

If there was one mantra echoed from coast to coast throughout the research it was that special educators did not go into the profession to give children the minimum required by law, but rather they entered teaching to benefit their students as much as possible. We appreciate the special education teachers and administrators who shared their perspectives with us. In no way, regardless of the conclusions drawn or recommendations made, should this book be interpreted as a condemnation of the work of America's special educators. Special educators work in a field that is quickly evolving around them with little voice in its evolution because their days are spent for the benefit of their students. These authors acknowledge and appreciate the work of America's special educators.

Many voices in this book are critical of practices and regulations that encompass special education. Other voices are critical of certain approaches to autism, and still others decry the growing political nature of special education advocacy. It takes listening to and sensitively portraying all of these voices to paint an accurate portrait of autism and special education today. Such a portrait is what we hope we offer in this book.

Chapter One

Unbundling, Mass Customization, and Public Policy

This is not something that's unique to the education market. This is a mega-trend of being able to provide mass customization—an individualized everything. It's not only possible, it's like gravity; it has to happen.

—Michael Moe

What is problematic is when something is put into code—be it state code or federal code. People pat themselves on the back and say, "Yes, this is good. Maybe we'll need to tweak it a little bit along the way, but we've got the basics."

—Greg Boris

Public education reflects the society it serves. In the past half century, the United States has transitioned, evolved, and morphed in ways that brought concurrent schoolhouse changes: from desegregation to transgender bathrooms, from Title I and the War on Poverty to Title IX and the battle for gender equality, from No Child Left Behind (NCLB) to the Every Student Succeeds Act (ESSA), from prayer out of schools to lockdown drills in the schools. Public education is not the master of its destiny but rather the mirror through which society reflects.

The societal changes manifested in our schools are far beyond the control of public education. Schools employ millions of teachers, administrators, and staff members who individually and collectively dedicate their professional lives to the well-being of their students. And each of those individuals knows the inefficiencies, bureaucracies, and idiocies that exist in the $630 billion

K–12 public school industry. Nonetheless, school professionals labor on, knowing their personal relationships with students leave a lifelong imprint regardless of the cacophony of policies, initiatives, and political drama that is the constant backdrop to their work.

This book addresses one of the fundamental components of public schooling—special education and its foundational law, the Individuals with Disabilities Education Act (IDEA). Just as external pressures brought into being IDEA's predecessor, Public Law 94-142 in 1975, so too external pressures challenge IDEA's administration and effectiveness. Despite its storied history and intent to champion the education of students with handicapping conditions, the process-oriented, regulation-intense, and weakly enforced law is growing increasingly antiquated in a field where research and political action, particularly around autism spectrum disorder (ASD), are eclipsing the law's intent and relevance.

In its next reauthorization, perhaps between 2017 and 2019, the law will need to respond to dramatic advances in technology as well as in behavioral sciences and neurosciences, but it will also be reassessed by an American society and political process that has dramatically changed since its last overhaul in 2004. The speed of change and the willingness to jettison the old, while frightening to some and invigorating to others, will color the next reauthorization and likely result in a very different law from the one of the past 40 years.

THE REALITY OF UNBUNDLING

The world is unbundling. On June 23, 2016, Great Britain voted to leave the European Union. Those who desired independence from the European Union wanted to break ties that would allow Great Britain greater ability to pass its own laws, set its own taxes, and control its own borders; this group defeated by a narrow margin those who desired greater economic ties to and open borders with the remainder of Europe. Great Britain's exit from the European Union is one of the most dramatic examples of the trend of unbundling, of simplifying, of rejecting ways of doing business that may have outlived their usefulness, and a return to a world where small is beautiful and proximity is newly appreciated.

America is unbundling. Millions of households have cut the cord to cable television. Who needs 150 channels when 99 percent of viewing is done on a handful of stations? Why pay for a package of television channels that includes material that is banal, salacious, or so ridiculous that you object to supporting it in order to watch classic movies or Orioles' baseball? Streaming services like Hulu, Amazon Prime, and Netflix provide viewers what they want when they want it, and a digital antenna provides plenty of free television for more and more households.

Music consumers no longer buy an album or a CD but rather purchase a single song. And that single song is less likely to be owned by a recording industry giant and more likely to be owned by an independent record label, by the songwriter, or by the performing artist. Services like Pandora and iHeartRadio create a custom mix of music based on individual preferences, and listeners have the ability to drop songs they do not want to hear.

There are perhaps a half dozen major breweries in the United States and an explosion of more than 4,000 craft breweries. Most Americans live within 10 miles of a brewery, and the nation enjoys more styles and brands of beer than any other country. Craft beer is celebrated in local, regional, and national festivals, and awards are given to the finest. Independent and customized have become a way of life, characteristics that more and more people value.

There are the "Big Five" in the publishing industry, and then there are the thousands of independent publishers, jointly releasing more than 2,000 books each business day. That number doubles when self-published books are included. The Big Five publishers are closed off and byzantine, unapproachable to 99 percent of America's writers. Independent publishers are regional or specialized and excited to find writers who match the focus of their press. Independent books are celebrated by award events that recognize the power of small presses to provide books that people value but fail to meet the expectations of the Big Five.

Whether it is beer, books, chocolate, bread, furniture, soap, or shirts, there is a distinct and ever-growing move to artisan-made versus mass-manufactured. It is a desire to know and be connected to the source, to the people who make the items or grow the food. It is a reflection of buying locally, knowing the food source, focusing on farm-to-table, and being aware of sweatshop conditions in a global economy.

America is monetizing in ways that challenge the 21st-century regulatory environment and harken back to the days of a cash economy. Internet communication connects buyers and sellers directly. One can buy or sell anything on eBay, hail a ride via Uber, book a room for the night at Airbnb, or arrange a vacation house for a month in Costa Rica with VRBO. These developments create countless challenges for traditional stores, taxis, and hotels and count-less headaches for government entities desiring to collect taxes and regulate.

America's 2016 presidential race witnessed a large-scale unbundling from the country's two major political parties. Bernie Sanders roiled the Democratic Party in his contest with Hillary Clinton, and Donald Trump persisted to a victory in the general election even though he alienated himself from the leadership of the Republican Party. The two-party system that has dominated American politics for more than a century is changing to an un-bundled landscape still under formation.

Americans are trending toward unbundled, mass-customized products. So, what does this have to do with public education? Simply put, public schools reflect the societies they serve, and America's public schools have responded to unbundling in a myriad of ways. But public school special education has been more constrained from reflecting the society it serves.

That constraint has primarily come from the highly process-oriented law that governs special education, the Individuals with Disabilities Education Act. But the unbundling process that is already manifested in mainstream K–12 public education will soon be reflected in the impregnable landscape of IDEA, with autism, the rise of applied behavior analysis (ABA), insurance mandates, and advocacy politics serving as the catalysts for change.

MASS CUSTOMIZATION

Through the 1990s, Michael Moe served as the guru of globalization for investment firms such as Merrill Lynch and Montgomery Securities. In the 21st century, Moe has founded and led two highly successful growth-stage investment companies, ThinkEquity and GSV Capital (GSV: Global Silicon Valley), where today he serves as CEO, Chief Investment Officer, and Chair-man of the Board.

For Moe, society's greatest challenge is ensuring that everyone has an equal opportunity to participate in the future and understanding that educa-tion is the fastest vehicle to that equality. As an ardent believer that educa-tion's fixation on nonprofit versus for-profit will soon yield to a focus on costs versus outcomes, his company has partnered with Arizona State Uni-versity since 2009 in sponsoring the ASU-GSV Summit, which brings the brightest minds, the deepest pockets, and the most visible education leaders together to think about how to create "Weapons of Mass Instruction."

Moe, hailed as one of the best minds in reading the confluence of social trends and technology, noted, "At ASU-GSV, an important ingredient is purposefully putting together people that come from different experiences, different jobs, and different roles: public education officials, teachers, principals, investors, entrepreneurs, policy officials, and business leaders. Typically these people would never be in the same room together. But when you put them in a room with that shared passion of accelerated innovation of education, great things come of it.

"Technology is the big enabler of the ability to have just-for-you, personalized products and services—truly mass customization. The concept has been with us for a while. You could sort of see where things were going and societal trends and so forth, but from a practical standpoint it remained difficult to do. But now with powerful adaptive technology and adaptive software, you're able in a very cost-effective, time-effective way to create just what the individual wants and needs.

"A fun example of that is going on in the automobile industry. To buy a Tesla you go online; you don't go to the dealership. Online you chose everything you want, from the tires to the seat covers to the stereo system. Technology now enables a mass customization process in what was traditionally a factory-type process. Our K–12 education system is a factory model. Students come in at kindergarten and get mustered out at 12th grade, provided they didn't get a defect along the way and get thrown out or didn't drop out. Unfortunately, lots of kids don't fit that factory model, or it doesn't help them be what they could be. The good news is that there is greater understanding that the factory model has lots of drawbacks. At the same time, technology is able to do things that are targeted and much more optimized for an individual child. That is a wonderfully positive thing, and now it's real, it's possible."

Moe continued, "When President Ford signed the special education law some 40 years ago, it was a major step forward. It was a start, a platform from which you build as scientific research and improved technology add to capacity. Common sense says that a kid with autism has different needs and requirements than a kid with dyslexia or a student who is developmentally delayed. To put them all in one group is not fair, and you don't need to do that. Today we are looking with fresh eyes at what can be done as opposed to what has been done.

"This is not a criticism of what has been done. That was a start, but now we look ahead. How do we match the needs of individual students and what they require—not the minimal accepted requirement, but the maximum, the optimized opportunity? And it's not about the money; it's about thinking in a fresh, better way. The tools, technologies, information, and insight are all available to give students resources to optimize their futures.

"The goal is about how to have students most effectively learn what they need to learn. They don't all need to be processed the same. We can unbundle, unshackle, but more importantly, provide the best experience for each student. This is not something that's unique to the education market. This is a megatrend of being able to provide mass customization—an individualized everything. It's not only possible, it's like gravity; it has to happen. You can try to push against it, but the force is so strong that it has to happen. It will happen."

Moe feels that the trends he sees in the capital markets also apply in the delivery of government services. "Fifteen or 20 years ago, I testified before Congress on educational technology. At that time you had one computer for every seven children and essentially no internet connectivity. The biggest impediment to adopting technology in the classroom was teachers, 85 percent of whom were uncomfortable using technology in the classroom. Today, people expect internet access everywhere, and they expect it to be wickedly fast; they expect devices to be ubiquitous, and they expect every kind of available software under the sun. And, by the way, they expect it for free, and this applies to public school teachers, too."

This relates to the special education world in Moe's view. "If you consider Uber and Airbnb, you see that change is inevitable. The taxi industry is big and the hotel industry is big, but it's gravity. People see firefights and regulatory threats and worry if Uber and Airbnb are going to be taken away. There is no possible way they're going to be taken away. The opponents are fighting against something that is inevitable.

"So you have $100 billion spent on the entrenched status quo of special education, and against it you have this army of advocates and passionate people determined to get the best education and treatments for children with special needs. I think it actually is part of this continuum of unbundling. The advocates are united via social media, which allows you to very rapidly organize around affinity, interest, and demographic with no relevance to geography. Social media and the internet, social mobile if you will, provide transparency in information, which is one of the beautiful things about the internet—creating better transparency, better information about what's out there, what can be done, what the costs are, and what the results are. In the case of these models like Uber that disrupt big, traditional industries, ultimately, it's gravity; it's a natural progression of progress" (Michael Moe, personal communication, July 19, 2016).

Ben Wallerstein is one of the nation's keenest minds on public policy and market trends. For 16 years he has worked at the intersection of Government Road and Free Enterprise Avenue. As cofounder of Whiteboard Advisors, his world is about bridging emerging ideas in education and health care and the public sector, bringing real-world solutions to real-world problems, and working with and around policies and bureaucracies that struggle to adjust or adapt to strategies, technologies, and delivery systems that fall outside of traditional practices and exceed the framework of existing regulation.

While Wallerstein shares much of Moe's enthusiasm for inevitability of change, he is grounded in the realities of public policy and sees the limits of the public purse. "The advocacy community has evolved dramatically between the 2004 reauthorization of IDEA and today. The intensity and sophistication of today's advocacy community is much greater. Philanthropic donors have come into the mix to support the special needs community in ways that are really positive. This creates the potential for some really interesting things to happen in the next reauthorization.

"It is important to bear in mind that public policy has to make tough trade-offs. In the education context in particular, we have to look at ourselves in the mirror and really question the extent and depth of innovation and outcomes that we're offering up. Programs that are significant and impactful and transformative—but are also really expensive—might not be as interesting from a public policy standpoint. Sometimes things move slowly and with good reason; it is tough to reallocate resources."

Wallerstein noted, "What is interesting to me are areas where policymakers are nonresponsive, and there's just a glaring moral imperative. Sometimes people think their issue presents a moral imperative but make the mistake of ignoring certain stakeholders or assuming an infinitely sized pie—and we don't have an infinitely sized pie. When you peel back the layers and think about the implications and externalities, there are far fewer policy 'no-brainers' than we might think. We often say that it is shameful that policymakers aren't moving in a particular direction. But you have to follow that to its logical conclusion. 'Should we do away with political redistricting?' Yes. 'Should we fix campaign finance in this country?' Absolutely. 'If we fix those, are we going to be on a pathway toward addressing a lot of the social issues that we care an awful lot about?' No doubt.

"What gets me really excited, and what I find promising about the success of companies like Uber and Airbnb is that when we really do have a break-through and transformative innovation, policy actually moves. It doesn't move as fast as we would all like it to move, but it moves. It's not always as bad as people think it is" (Ben Wallerstein, personal communication, July 19, 2016).

"It is a long slog between the germ of an idea and the realization of that idea in terms of legislation," noted Greg Boris, former public school special education administrator, professor, lobbyist, and current Senior Leadership Development and Policy Specialist at the University of South Dakota Center for Disabilities. "Teddy Roosevelt was the first person who talked about federal mandates on health care. More than a century later we finally get the Affordable Care Act. Whether you like it or not, it took more than a hundred years to have something happen. With respect to people with disabilities, we had court decisions in the 1950s that told school districts that they have to educate all kids. But those were in federal district court or appellate court, and it did not hit at a national level. And it wasn't until 1975 that it came through in terms of federal legislation. Litigation led the way to legislation.

"What is problematic is when something is put into code—be it state code or federal code. People pat themselves on the back and say, 'Yes, this is good. Maybe we'll need to tweak it a little bit along the way, but we've got the basics.' But what people see as potential for individuals labeled as disabled has changed markedly in the last 20 years. Nonetheless, our legislative system is reluctant to go back and do a wholesale overhaul of the law. Instead we tweak the process we have in place; we improve it incrementally and smooth out the rough edges. We've had some good tweaks along the way, like the early childhood amendments and even the language amendments changing it from 'handicapped children' to 'individuals with disabilities.' But there are some areas that need more than tweaking."

Boris continued, "What we have structured in federal law does not account for changes in pedagogy or changes in medical knowledge or changes in human knowledge on how to address any one of the 13 disability categories. It says, 'Here are the categories, and you get your multidisciplinary team, you do the assessment, you identify the present levels of performance, you note strengths and weaknesses, you write IEPs, et cetera.' It doesn't allow for changes. It's what we're stuck with.

"The last thing I wanted when I was a college professor was to see one of my former student's name in the paper for being sued. I wanted them to do the right thing, legally at minimum, for the kids. At the same time I wanted them to be doing right by kids. Doing right by kids often means going beyond the minimum. You cannot legislate maximums, but you can certainly legislate minimums. That is the shortcoming of the law as we know it. What we knew about autism 20 years ago, when we were talking about 1 in 1,000 children, or whatever the numbers were, has changed dramatically. How we address autism has changed dramatically. Our technology has changed dramatically, but our special education systems that surround autism have remained static" (Greg Boris, personal communication, June 15, 2015).

SETTING THE COURSE FOR THE BOOK

This book explores how societal changes, the explosion of the number of children with autism, the growing profession of applied behavior analysis, and the increasingly politically aggressive positions of advocacy groups will influence the reauthorization of IDEA. Chapter 2 shows how public education has responded to the pressures of unbundling and mass customization. It also shows how special education has not been able to make similar changes and discusses the resultant singular disability framework that is taking shape.

Chapter 3 relays the stories of autism parents and advocates who have traveled unique roads and, as a result, have different visions of the politics of autism and the role of special education. Chapter 4 describes how autism has become the catalyst that will change IDEA. It also examines the rise of Autism Speaks and its impact on the autism advocacy and dyslexia advocacy worlds, demonstrating how political relief focused on a specific disability is changing the landscape. The disconnection between the day-to-day world of autism families and the structures of special education are portrayed in chapter 5. While special education has a noble purpose, government programs are hard-pressed to keep up with the rapid development in related sciences and the case law that is reshaping IDEA.

Chapter 6 explores the practice of applied behavior analysis from its clinical origins in the late 1980s to its formation as a profession. The chapter includes voices that disagree with ABA as the preferred treatment for children with autism. Personal stories that demonstrate the gap between theory and practice in special education are the focus of chapter 7, and chapter 8 focuses on the disconnection in services and looks at how three exemplary programs are responding to the increase in autism and the rise of the profession of applied behavior analysis. The book concludes with chapter 9's compilation of recommendations offered by the many voices in the book and proposes additional considerations for reauthorization.

Chapter Two

Market Forces, Special Education, and Lost Intensity

The heart of what we do in special education is customization.

—Michelle Powers

Schools no longer can provide intensive instruction.

—Douglas Fuchs

Public education is often referred to as a monolithic, one-size-fits-all provider of schooling. And it is, if you are looking at the forest and not the trees. But stare at those trees for a moment and you will see that decades of efforts in response to changes in society and efforts to maintain market share are found among the branches and leaves.

Just within the "Reform Era," which began in 1983 with President Reagan's Blue Ribbon Commission report, *A Nation at Risk*, most states and school districts have changed some long-held fundamentals. Open enrollment is an adjustment that began during the mid-1980s, allowing students to enroll in schools other than the one for which they are "zoned." So, if a third grader is zoned to attend Washington Elementary School, but her mother works in an office across the street from Adams Elementary, mom can register her daughter at Adams under open enrollment.

There are rules and timetables that must be honored, but open enrollment is an accommodation, an effort to offer flexibility to the old rule of having the home address determine the school assignment. There is intradistrict and interdistrict open enrollment. So, not only are traditional zoning lines within a district fading, if not vanishing, district boundaries are also becoming more permeable.

District-operated charter schools are another accommodation to offering options for families, as are public schools with a special theme or curriculum such as technical schools, language immersion schools, or single gender schools. Public schools make efforts to provide choices that meet their communities' needs. Online course offerings, alternative schools, part-time enrollment of homeschooled students, and dual enrollment opportunities allowing high school students to earn college credits are examples of public education's efforts to offer a variety of opportunities where many sizes fit the various needs of many families.

The rationale for each of these accommodations varies from state to state and district to district. In general, the moves are responses to market forces, to families having a growing choice of options, to non-district charters popping up, and to online schools erasing borders and enrolling kids. The moves have not been made in a proactive let's-give-families-more-choice sense, but in a reactive we-better-do-this-or-we'll-lose-market-share sense. Nonetheless, these options have expanded the framework of public education while maintaining its domination of the market and its position as a major community resource.

Throughout the three decades of expanding options within public schools, special education has more or less stayed the course. Students with disabilities operate under an Individualized Education Program (IEP) and remain connected to the "traditional" model of public schooling, with the array of choice options virtually meaningless for students in most states. If IDEA guarantees students an individualized program in which parents carry veto power, why would a parent look elsewhere? Because special education, once the mother of customization, is now mired by regulations, oblivious to outcomes, and hardly the innovative force it once was in its early days.

The exceptions to the rule that special education students have been left out of the options created for mainstream students exist in Florida and in 10 other states. In 1999, Florida enacted the McKay Scholarship Program for Students with Disabilities. The McKay Scholarship was created because Florida State Senator John McKay struggled with his local public school special education program to get appropriate services for his child. He reasoned that if it was such a struggle for him, a top elected state official, to get appropriate special education services for his child, it must be much more challenging for a typical Florida family.

The McKay program provides a voucher for eligible special education students to attend a participating private school. During the 2015–2016 school year, more than 31,000 Florida students utilized the McKay Scholarship, and another 10 states have since developed some form of a McKay-like voucher program for students with IEPs.

As GSV CEO Michael Moe noted, "I knew Uber had it made when politicians were taking Uber rides too. They loved Uber just as much as everybody else did. I'm not saying everything should be free market and that nothing should be provided for by the government, not at all. But I think the government is better when there are alternatives. When there is no competition across the street, what you typically get is inefficient, expensive, and of mediocre quality, which in the case of education has pretty disastrous consequences.

"When the U.S. Postal Service was created, it was a critical service necessary to advance society and commerce. God bless the U.S. Postal Service, but if FedEx and UPS had not come along, what would the U.S. Postal Service have done? I don't think you would be seeing U.S. mail trucks driving around the neighborhood on Sundays" (Michael Moe, personal communication, July 19, 2016).

But in 80 percent of the states, there are no McKay-like programs for those with an IEP, and in states across the country, the law itself, or at least the manner in which it is implemented, constrains opportunities that can benefit a child, according to Daniel Unumb, a nationally recognized autism law expert and former director of the Autism Speaks Legal Resource Center. "There is a lack of options, and that lack of choice is compounded by the way these separate institutional systems—education, health care, behavioral health care, and vocational training—are set up. They are not formulated and integrated to the benefit of the child, which they really need to be.

"There have been more options created for typical children, but for a child with autism, which can be a global deficit impacting all aspects of the child's life, the system limits choice and even works against the needs of the child. Take a case where a child needs a certain intensive intervention that must be delivered in a variety of settings at an intensity of hours to be effective. If it is delivered in that manner, the child has an excellent chance of becoming substantially or fully functional and of having a very productive life. But all too often schools prevent access to those therapies because they won't allow a health care provider in to ensure that generalization is occurring in the school, which is a large chunk of a child's day."

Unumb continued, "Too often, schools won't allow the necessary coordination among the funding streams. So the parent is left with the choice to either send their child to public school and have them forgo that critical intervention for that huge chunk of the child's time or to pull the child out of school altogether and find a private setting or homeschooling. They forgo what was intended in terms of access to IDEA intervention and support so that they can get the necessary health care they need to actually improve their child's disability and substantially ameliorate it. Parents should not be in that situation. That is not educational choice."

Choice is further limited, in Unumb's view, for families with children in special education because of the dearth of information and performance indicators available. "With my neurotypical kid, I can go to a school and say, 'What do your test scores look like? How many kids do you place in postsecondary education? What is your graduation rate?' All of these key statistical data points are available. But a parent cannot get comparable data from special education. Questions such as 'How many kids do you have who start out as nonverbal, who then are talking and communicating in a full fashion by the time they graduate?' or 'How many kids do you have with autism that will graduate with employable skills?' go largely unanswered. The school district will respond, 'Well, it's all individualized. Every child is different, and therefore, we don't know.' These are questions that a school district should be able to answer" (Daniel Unumb, personal communication, July 18, 2016).

WHY DO WE HAVE SPECIAL EDUCATION?

Those whose public education careers began prior to 1977 worked in an environment that predated federal law that guaranteed the right to an education for students with disabilities. Special education came about because public school districts refused admission to more than 1 million children with handicapping conditions and badly underserved millions more. And, as any review of the history will reveal, all of this happened in the working life of the senior members of today's education cadre.

State and federal support for special education predates the advent of American public education by 30 some years. Horace Mann's Tenth and Twelfth annual reports to the Massachusetts Board of Education, in 1846 and 1848 respectively, are considered the launching pad for universal public education in the United States. However, the founding of the American Asylum for the Education of the Deaf and Dumb in 1817 was supported by an appropriation of $5,000 from the Connecticut legislature in 1816 and a grant of 23,000 acres of land from the federal government in 1819 (Alexander and Alexander 2012, 561).

But the establishment of what is now the American School for the Deaf in West Hartford was not typical of the opportunities provided to children with handicapping conditions during the first 125 years of American public schooling. Despite Horace Mann's dedication to the needs of the mentally ill in the 1820s and 1830s, as public education gathered steam across the country, severely challenged students in a vast majority of states were excluded, and in some states, laws prevented the parents of handicapped children from attempting to enroll their children in public schools (Alexander and Alexander 2012, 562).

"Until the mid-1970s, laws in most states allowed school districts to refuse to enroll any student they considered 'uneducable,' a term generally defined by local school administrators" (Martin, Martin, and Terman 1996, 26). In the 1960s, advocates for those with handicapping conditions made headway within the federal government. The Civil Rights Movement and President Lyndon Johnson's Great Society, his vision for the eradication of poverty and elimination of discrimination, provided a framework for further action by advocacy groups. In 1966, Congress authorized the Bureau for the Education of the Handicapped (BEH). "As separate programs for the disabled—and earmarked portions of general education programs—proliferated, the BEH recommended that many existing federal programs be codified into a more comprehensive Education of the Handicapped Act (EHA). In 1970, Congress passed the EHA" (Martin et al. 1996, 27).

Despite the federal action and an increasing number of state laws focused on the education of children with handicapping conditions, millions of children remained unserved or underserved. "A significant turning point for the special-needs children's rights occurred in 1971, when a federal district court ruled that retarded children in Pennsylvania are entitled to a free, public education" (Alexander and Alexander 2012, 562). "In the following year, in *Mills v. Board of Education*, seven children between the ages of 8 and 16 with a variety of mental and behavioral disabilities brought suit against the District of Columbia public schools, which had refused to enroll some students and expelled others, solely on the basis of their disability. The school district admitted that an estimated 12,340 children with disabilities within the district's boundaries would not be served during the 1971–72 school year because of budget constraints" (Martin et al. 1996, 28).

The Pennsylvania decision (*Pennsylvania Association for Retarded Children v. Commonwealth of Pennsylvania*) and the *Mills* decision provided crucial precedents; dozens of federal court decisions were based on their principles in the next two years. Congressional hearings in 1975 revealed that "3.5 million children with disabilities in the country were not receiving an education appropriate to their needs, while almost 1 million more were receiving no education at all" (Martin et al. 1996, 29).

First introduced in 1975, the Education for All Handicapped Children Act (Public Law 94-142) passed in Congress by an overwhelming majority (only 14 representatives and senators voted against it) and was signed into law by President Gerald Ford in late November 1975 with implementation scheduled for October 1, 1977 (Martin et al. 1996, 30). President Ford made this statement upon signing: "Unfortunately, this bill promises more than the Federal Government can deliver, and its good intentions could be thwarted by the many unwise provisions it contains" (Freedman 2012, 2).

President Ford's comment was prescient. From the get-go, the federal mandate lacked specificity, relied on case law for clarification, and was woefully underfunded. Public Law 94-142 was based on *Brown v. Board of Education of Topeka* and guaranteed access to public education for children with disabilities. But despite all the good intentions, the law still had to be administered, and a bureaucracy was created that focused more on process than outcome, lost sight of its original intent, and failed to keep up with the research. After 40 years of regulation upon regulation and calculated noncompliance on the part of school districts, this parentally enforced federal law is ripe for unbundling.

Sonja Kerr is an attorney at Cuddy Law Firm, P.L.L.C., a special education law practice with offices in New York, Texas, and Ohio. The fact that parents, whether through direct interaction with school districts or through legal action, are the enforcers of IDEA infuriates Kerr. Equally frustrating, in Kerr's view, is the fact that parents are placed in untenable financial situations at the calculated judgment of school districts, which leads to what she sees as the private enforcement of a federal mandate.

Kerr noted, "IDEA is one of the few federally mandated programs that has very little enforcement by the United States Department of Education and Department of Justice. If you compare, for example, environmental law and the EPA or other regulated industries, we have some case law where the federal departments of regulation for the EPA have acted on behalf of individuals who are meant to be protected by the law. But we have left nearly all of the enforcement responsibility for special education to the private sector and the private bar, including private attorneys and public interest attorneys.

"That seems to me to be impacting the way in which the law is developing in a couple ways. One is that families who do not have means, a large portion of the 6 million children in the United States, are not really receiving the representation that they need. On a good day, there are maybe 1,500 special education parent-side attorneys across the country. This means that we have an imbalance in the enforcement that's been left to the private sector, because I can't even think of a school district that would not have an attorney who knows something about special education law either in-house or on retainer.

"We've created an imbalance. For instance, in Pennsylvania we have 500 school districts, and every one of those school districts has a solicitor or a contract with a private attorney who knows special education while the parents are left to fend for themselves. In Pennsylvania—a state that has considerably more parent-side bar in comparison to other states—you may find 75 to 90 parent-side attorneys on a good day. There is a huge imbalance, and that plays out."

Kerr explained, "That plays out in terms of not only individual children, but it plays out in terms of systems because schools can make determinations of, 'Well, we're going to operate this way or that way.' And even if someone wonders if 'this way or that way' is marginally acceptable legally, there's a tendency for school districts to think, 'Well, let's just see what happens and if anyone complains.' So, unless there is pushback, unless there is resistance, unless parents and parent-side bar and advocates step up, there is widespread noncompliance.

"Every report prepared by the National Council on Disability has shown widespread noncompliance in relation to IDEA, and it's not just limited to noncompliance on paper. We can see the results. We can see the results in the very high unemployment rate of children who graduate from our special education programs. They do not have the requisite skills to work, they do not have the means to get into and stay in postsecondary programs, and so they are generally falling further behind.

"People have to pay penalties. People lose their right to practice for a certain period of time if, for example, they are a stockbroker and have violated the law. But if you ruin a child's life because you failed to provide the services that were needed at the appropriate time, what happens at most is that the school is required to provide make-up services or a better program and pay some amount of attorney's fees, which are usually covered by the district's insurance."

Kerr continued, "There is a need for special education reform. When you see, as we have since 1976, the numbers of children whose parents have mortgaged their homes, who have moved from state to state, who have gone to state legislatures or to Congress, to the courts, to the media, or to anyone who would listen to say, 'My kid is not getting what the IDEA promised,' I don't think that the problem is the cottage industry of special education attorneys or advocacy groups. I think the problem is that school districts have probably done a cost-benefit analysis. They have looked at it and said, 'Well, we have a school district of 3,000 kids, and we have 700 students with IEPs. Let's just say that 50 of them complain during the school year; that will cost us 'x' amount of dollars, so we'll just build that into our budget.' Special education is a noncompliant compliance-driven model" (Sonja Kerr, personal communication, December 16, 2015).

THE SINGULAR DISABILITY FRAMEWORK

Federal involvement in special education opened the schoolhouse doors for more than a million children denied access. It also created what has become a $100 billion component of public schooling. Special education overflows with caring people who are engulfed in a system ruled by process. Meeting the needs of each individual child is a noble goal. But while there are 6.5 million IEPs in place, they are not handcrafted or artisan made. A vast majority of the programs within a district hardly vary one from another and are composed of the ingredients available within the local district or an interdistrict cooperative.

While it is true that some IEPs are monstrous in detail, complexity, and volume, the vast majority are routinely designed and executed. For instance, Brewster's IEP specifies 20 minutes of speech each week, daily resource support in the library for 30 minutes, and a weekly visit with the social worker, while Bonita's calls for 20 minutes with a speech-language pathologist (SLP) twice a week, daily resource support for a full hour, and a monthly check-in with the social worker. The students' IEPs simply contain different amounts of the same ingredients. And if Brewster or Bonita changes school districts or even schools within the same district, the IEP will not travel with them, but will be reconstituted with the ingredients available at the new school.

In movements, be they for racial equity, gender equity, or homeschooling, there are generally three types of participants: pioneers, settlers, and recreational vehicle owners. Pioneers risk their lives for the cause; they go to jail, get bloodied, and they take and hold ground. Settlers follow, organizing the newly taken land and setting up systems and services to make it functional. Recreational vehicle owners arrive last, seeking all the conveniences of life and having little understanding of and appreciation for those who came before them. It is this generation of special education advocates, the recreational vehicle owners, which considers a special education law that bundles handicapping conditions into a single procedure as both antiquated and irrelevant.

The singular disability framework is the special education equivalent of cutting the cable television cord. Parents are organizing to make sure that their children are served, that their disability gets what is needed, and that their insurance program picks up where the IEP stops. It is every disability for itself. It is a recreational vehicle state of mind.

Michelle Powers knows a great deal about special education and IEPs. She has served as the South Dakota Department of Education Director of Special Education, is the current Director of Special Education for the Brookings, South Dakota, School District, and is the mother of a child with an IEP. "The heart of what we do in special education is customization. If schools genuinely get to a level of customization that meets the needs of the students and includes designed instructional approaches based on where kids are individually, we will not need special education.

"There are many demands placed on educators today in terms of their knowledge base. Compared to when I started almost 30 years ago, the special education knowledge base today is much more sophisticated. There are many more demands and much greater expectations placed on special education.

"As with so many important social issues today, we're in a different place. As special educators, we are more knowledgeable and we are more skilled. But at the end of the day, public schools get a certain amount of dollars, and they figure out how to make it all work. Districts will make the choices they are allowed to make. I understand why districts make the decisions they do. They would do it all if they could. I genuinely believe that" (Michelle Powers, personal communication, June 10, 2016).

Gina Green, a practitioner, researcher, and executive director of the Association of Professional Behavior Analysts (APBA), takes issue with the hodge-podge nature of most IEPs. "IDEA has institutionalized a multidisciplinary treatment model that sounds all nice and warm and fuzzy, but what it means in reality very often is that kids end up getting very fragmented and eclectic intervention. It's like all of the professionals have to have a piece of the child. So the speech therapist has to have a piece and the occupational therapists get their piece and the classroom teachers get their piece. There's no cohesion; there's no unified, consistent framework for intervention. There's no single, qualified expert or professional who is overseeing the intervention.

"You have speech pathologists using various techniques in their offices, some of which may not be very scientific. You have occupational therapists doing whatever they do, some of whom use techniques that have not been validated scientifically. Then in the special education or regular education classrooms, students are getting a mishmash of different interventions, many of which have never been tested scientifically or may have been tested and proven to be ineffective."

Green noted, "There are a number of studies on the mixed-method, eclectic intervention model that result in kids with autism getting a little bit of this and little bit of that; some professionals even do things that actually countermand and are counterproductive to proven techniques. Not surprisingly, the studies show that this doesn't work. Most kids do not make much progress in that kind of multidisciplinary, eclectic intervention. But it's so entrenched in the public schools that it is really difficult to get around it" (Gina Green, personal communication, July 14, 2015).

Douglas Fuchs is Professor and Nicholas Hobbs Chair in Special Education and Human Development at Peabody College of Vanderbilt University and is a member of the Vanderbilt Kennedy Center for Research on Human Development. Discussing autism's impact on special education, the growth of applied behavior analysis, and prospects for the reauthorization of IDEA stems from his life's work. "This is a great topic; it really is a great topic for a lot of reasons. The wheels hopefully won't come off of public education, but the wheels are beginning to wobble because more and more people see the schools as incapable of providing the kind of intervention that their children need. Board Certified Behavior Analysts represent an effort to jack up the intensity of services that many, many kids—we're talking hundreds of thousands, if not millions—with a variety of labels requiring intensive instruction are not getting, period. They are not getting it.

"Twenty and 30 years ago or 30 and 40 years ago, special education saw itself as the provider of intensive instruction. I'm not trying to paint a rosy picture of the good old days, but there was an acknowledgment, there was recognition, there was an identity that said special educators were the people who were responsible for delivering this kind of intensive instruction, which by definition would not be found in general education. For all kinds of reasons, including an inclusion movement that, in my view, took an unfortunate turn—meaning that inclusion turned into a kind of orthodox full inclusion—and for lots of other reasons, schools no longer can provide intensive instruction" (Douglas Fuchs, personal communication, July 16, 2015).

STATIC VERSUS DYNAMIC DISABILITY

When Congress passed Public Law 94-142, it was focused on the million children who were excluded from schools and on the lack of quality services for severely challenged children who were enrolled in public schools. The law was passed to right a wrong; it was wrong, and it became illegal after the law, to exclude children from school because of a disability. The law was written for access—all children are entitled to a public education. But the law was not written for benefit. Public Law 94-142 did not set academic, social, or behavioral expectations. The law watched after the outcomes for children by giving parents an unprecedented role in designing and approving the program for their children.

Giving parents a voice in their child's IEP was an amazing feat. Congress knew that parents were not educators and that many parents lacked an adequate education themselves. But Congress also knew that parents love their children. Giving parents a voice was revolutionary in 1975 and still remarkable in 1985. But the complexities of having mom and dad engaged in the IEP process mounted as the number of children covered under the law grew to more than 6 million. Providing access, the original intent of the law, became the sole application of the law. Demonstrating compliance with the law became the administrative raison d'être.

The law that granted access became an administrative nightmare. So much attention was devoted to fearing the regulatory beast that special education became a maintenance system for students whose disabilities remained static. Serving the students was mandatory; improving their lot in life was not.

By 1995 and certainly by 2005, special education was significantly out of step with the rapidly developing behavioral sciences and neurosciences, which view disabilities as dynamic. These sciences are part of the medical model, which seeks maximum benefit or cure from its treatments. Maximum benefit for children with handicapping conditions was not required of special education per the *Board of Education of the Hendrick Hudson Central School District v. Rowley* 1982 U.S. Supreme Court decision. Cure? Teachers were not doctors, and the word cure was not in their vocabulary or in their special education training.

Enter the recreational vehicle owners who connected the dots between the behavioral sciences and neurosciences and the IEP process. When they determined that the trajectory of their children's lives could be substantially elevated by developments in the sciences, they put more pressure on special education and took their battle to insurance companies, enlisting the support of lawmakers to make sure their children were the beneficiaries of every piece of research, every technological development, every behavioral and education technique, and every insurance and tax dollar available.

As a prime example of connecting the dots, applied behavior analysis emerged in recent decades as an effective treatment for children with autism. While it is not the only treatment, its foundation in behavioral science and body of related research provide it top status among families and recognition by health insurers, the United States Department of Health and Human Services, and the American Academy of Pediatrics.

Applied behavior analysis is designed and supervised by a Board Certified Behavior Analyst (BCBA), and the intensity that an ABA program can demand challenges the structures of special education. This relatively new profession has risen outside the purview of state departments of education and outside of traditional public education licensure and control mechanisms. Public schools employ only a sliver of the 20,000 BCBAs in the nation, but the emergence of the applied behavior analysis profession and the appearance of recreational vehicle drivers have set the stage for the unbundling of IDEA.

REFERENCES

Alexander, K. and Alexander, M. D. 2012. *American Public School Law*. 8th edition. Belmont, CA: Wadsworth, Cengage Learning.

Freedman, M. K. 2012. "Special Education: Its Ethical Dilemmas, Entitlement Status, and Suggested Systemic Reforms." *The University of Chicago Law Review* 79(1): 1–24: Online Exclusive. Retrieved from https://lawreview.uchicago.edu/sites/lawreview.uchicago.edu/files/uploads/79_1/Freedman.pdf.

Martin, E. W., Martin, R., and Terman, D. 1996. "The Legislative and Litigation History of Special Education." *The Future of Children: Special Education for Students with Disabilities* 6(1): 25–39.

Chapter Three

Public Schools and Autism, It Gets Very Personal

Access to services shouldn't depend on your bank balance or your zip code.

—Judith Ursitti

Public Law 94-142 was extraordinary, and I still have a place in my heart that says this is *the* law of the 20th century.

—Sheryl Dicker

Andrew and Judith Ursitti moved a number of times during the first 10 years of their marriage. Andrew's job took them to Chicago, Atlanta, and the D.C. area. When they were transferred to Southlake, Texas, the Ursittis knew they were home. The necessary relocations to advance in the corporate world were now finished, and they were ready to raise their children in the Lone Star State.

Judith Ursitti grew up in Texas. "I did not come from an affluent family, but I was the prom queen, the most likely to succeed, and had every opportunity because my brain functioned typically. Our son was diagnosed with autism at age 2, and he's more severely affected on the spectrum. I know the loving, good side of my home state. It's just a God-fearing culture. But on the other hand, we lived in Southlake, where the school district had a $16 million football stadium but wouldn't provide any sort of support for my severely affected son. The local school system slammed the door in his face. They did everything they could to make it impossible for us to keep him in the public school. They offered to put him in an inclusive classroom with kids who were English as a second language learners—one teacher and 20 kids. That was certainly not what he needed at 3 years old.

"I am not a combative person. I'm not one who wants to fight with the schools or stomp into the principal's office; that's not me. But what happened to my son was a total wake-up call."

That wake-up call moved Ursitti to become a warrior for children with autism. As the current Director of State Government Relations for Autism Speaks, her battleground is state legislatures, where she has promoted autism coverage under health insurance plans. And her exasperation with the South-lake public schools largely dissipated when her husband was transferred to Massachusetts.

When her son was 4 and had been in the Dover, Massachusetts, public schools for a few months, the special education director came to Ursitti and said, "We can't meet his needs. We need to start looking at programs that can." Ursitti and district personnel toured private programs around the state. She recalled, "When it came time to decide which program would be appropriate, the school district made a recommendation, but the IEP team said to me, and I will never forget this, they said, 'It's your decision; you're the parent, you know best.' So he ended up going to the program I felt was the best fit for him. He's been going there for years. It's a wonderful program, and he's lucky to have a spot there."

With the education piece set, Ursitti worked to put the medical piece in place. "When we were in Texas our pediatrician was excellent, but there were no developmental pediatricians. Good medical support in Texas was just unavailable. There was no one to see to help guide you. But here in Boston, we have the Lurie Center for Autism, which is affiliated with Massachusetts General Hospital. My son has a team of doctors who've supported him through the years with different medical issues that are tough to identify because he has such a severe communication disorder. The medical team also works very closely with his IEP team, so all those services are coordinated."

Ursitti continued, "In Texas, the educational model did not fit with the treatments that our pediatrician and neurologist were prescribing. It was just a complete disconnect. It's that thing where the school says, 'We don't do that, that's medical.' And the health care providers say, 'We don't do that, that's educational.' Families fall into this pit where they have to do private pay because no one is offering the appropriate services. In Texas, a lot of families end up pulling their kids out of the public school program, doing therapies at home, and homeschooling for the educational component. Here in Massachusetts, my son has his health care services and he has his IEP-based services, and they are all in sync. Massachusetts is nirvana when you look at that model."

Back in Texas, after her son was diagnosed with autism, Ursitti "turned on the *Today Show* and they were doing a week-long series on autism. Every day they had a different report. One day Bob and Suzanne Wright were on, and that's how I learned about Autism Speaks, the organization the Wrights started. I was a mom in Southlake, Texas, watching this, but there were millions of moms all over the country watching. It encouraged me. It empowered me. The Wrights truly changed everything. People now know what autism is, and they are not afraid to talk about it. There is greater understanding because the Wrights were open and worked so hard."

As Autism Speaks' Director of State Government Relations, Ursitti focuses on legislation requiring autism to be covered under health plans. Her personal experience was typical of what many families have found. "I am advocating for something specific—health insurance coverage for evidence-based treatment for autism—because autism has been specifically singled out and excluded. I experienced this when my son was diagnosed. It said in our health plan that it does not cover autism. Autism is a specific problem that requires a specific solution.

"The basic requirement of the Individuals with Disabilities Education Act for students with qualifying disabilities is to access the curriculum, it's not to ameliorate the symptoms of the disorder or disease or condition. IEP-based services are designed to help students access the curriculum. But in a vast majority of states, you are not going to have very robust IEP-based services to begin with. In New York you can get ABA-based services through an IEP. In the Northeast it's more likely. But in the flyover states, it's falling more into the medical model because that's where the funding is for ABA. I don't think the Massachusetts model will ever be replicated in other parts of the country because other states just refuse to fund school-based services."

Ursitti explained, "I just spent 48 hours in Oklahoma, and it's a great example of what I am talking about. It is a no-man's-land. Families do not get any sort of applied behavior analysis in the school systems there. We've tried to pass autism insurance in Oklahoma but have not been successful. But we're looking again to see if we can find a way to move forward to get a funding stream going so families can access quality care, just the basic evidence-based care for their loved ones with autism.

"Getting meaningful intervention to kids on the autism spectrum comes through health insurance, through the medical model. IDEA has never been fully funded, and the way it is written is just not going to compel most school districts to do the right thing" (Judith Ursitti, personal communication, August 6, 2015). Oklahoma has since passed autism insurance legislation.

The implementation of Public Law 94-142 in 1977 opened the schoolhouse gate for more than 1 million children previously excluded or minimally served. Like many federal laws, the intent was to provide a guarantee, to ensure a right, and to override the attitudes of exclusion found in so many locations. Sheryl Dicker was in the field prior to Public Law 94-142. "Before 94-142, we had a tradition in New York law that allowed us—it was so stupid and ridiculous—it allowed us to go to family court and get an order for special education. Then the social workers would find some basement place where a kid could go to school. I also saw firsthand children who were 10, 11, 12 years old who had never been to school. In Syracuse, New York, there were kids in attics in 1974, kids who never went outside, kids who were not going to school. So for me the passing of Public Law 94-142 was extraordinary, and I still have a place in my heart that says this is *the* law of the 20th century."

Dicker has spent her career working as an advocate for children and adults with special needs. She has served as a special education attorney and child services administrator on the local, state, and federal levels. She has also been a professor in the pediatrics department of Albert Einstein College of Medicine, was general counsel for the Arkansas Department of Human Services, and served 16 years as executive director of the New York State Permanent Judicial Commission on Justice for Children. Her professional experience is deep and extensive. She is also the mother of a daughter on the spectrum.

"My daughter was born in 1991, and we were struggling during the '90s and nobody—and I mean nobody in Washington, and I was on the President's Committee on Mental Retardation—none of these experts spotted the possibility that my daughter could be on the spectrum. She spoke late, she walked late, she had behavioral issues; there were red flags all over the place. But it was the '90s and it wasn't clear. It wasn't until 2002 that the thought that she might be PDD came up, and then the special education people and I worked accordingly. My daughter earned a regular high school diploma that enabled her to secure any job requiring one and to go to college. My daughter is a former teacher's aide in a Devereux school that uses an ABA model. That would have been unlikely with an IEP diploma."

Dicker continued, "But to think back to the passage of 94-142, there were thousands of us who were implementing that law all over the country. I was first in Philadelphia and then in Arkansas, and it was just an incredible thing to be part of this exciting movement from 1975 until the early '80s. It wasn't very hard, frankly, to be a lawyer or an advocate for those kids because the law was so clear and the regulations were so clear, and no one argued with us really. It was a very exciting time. The focus those first seven or eight years of the law were very much on access."

Dicker noted, "In *Springdale v. Sherry Grace* in the early '80s, the Springdale School District said all deaf children had to go to the Arkansas School for the Deaf, which was in Little Rock, 150 miles away. So we argued for a regional program so that my client, Sherry, a little 6-year-old, wouldn't have to leave home and live in a dorm. Those are the kinds of issues we dealt with, and it was a pleasure. It wasn't that controversial. It wasn't hard. It was a pleasure because at the end of the day, everybody seemed happy with the results. And then in 1982, *Rowley* (U.S. Supreme Court decision stating that schools had to only provide a basic floor of opportunity under Public Law 94-142) was a stopping point. *Rowley* stopped, at least for me, that good feeling that this is easy, that everyone would listen. It was a significant turning point. *Rowley* changed the point of view. School districts became tougher."

Dicker was among thousands of advocates stunned by the *Rowley* decision. "I got a call from a reporter in 1982 when *Rowley* was decided. The reporter said, 'I'm calling for your comments about the Supreme Court decision in *Rowley*.' And I said, 'Oh, great!' And he said, 'I don't think you know what the decision was.' And I didn't because I was sure that *Rowley* was going to win. That was my point of view and that of both the special education people and lawyers with whom I worked in the early '80s" (Sheryl Dicker, personal communication, July 31, 2015).

Rowley was a pivot point for former Autism Speaks' attorney Daniel Unumb as well. "It's a square peg in a round hole. The *Rowley* decision, where the primary issue was access to education, was fairly narrowly conceived and not as much on the substantive aspect of what does a meaningful education consist of, particularly in light of a child's capabilities and possibilities. *Rowley* itself was very specific to the facts before the Court, but because it is a Supreme Court case, it came to be used by the circuits in a broader, more blunt fashion than was probably intended.

"When you identify that there have been tremendous advances in terms of both the interventions available to people with disabilities and technology for people with disabilities, the potential for people with disabilities to lead meaningful, functional lives has increased. Some of that language has been picked up in subsequent authorizations of IDEA, talking about the importance of preparing children with disabilities for further education, employment, and independent living. But the actual mechanisms to do that, which are available, have not been broadly available through the public education system. So, there's been a tremendous amount of tension as a result of that."

Unumb noted, "*Rowley* really needs to be revisited because we are paying the price every day for not sufficiently educating our children with disabilities and for not allowing them to live the most functional lives possible, which would dramatically decrease the burden on our social safety net system, if you will, and dramatically increase the ability of these children to live lives as we know it. I think that there is a tremendous amount of pressure from parents and advocacy groups. We need to step up to the modern-day realities and provide a meaningful education for people with disabilities" (Daniel Unumb, personal communication, July 18, 2016).

Daniel Unumb and his wife, Lorri Unumb, are attorneys and colleagues of Judith Ursitti. In response to the journey with their son on the spectrum, the Unumbs have become two of the most vocal and visible advocates for health insurance to cover evidence-based treatment for children with autism. Along with other advocates, the Unumbs helped South Carolina become the second state to pass a law mandating this type of health insurance coverage in 2007. By mid-2016, 44 states had enacted such measures, with no small part played by the Unumbs and Ursitti of Autism Speaks.

Sheryl Dicker, Judith Ursitti, and Daniel and Lorri Unumb are all national figures and champions for those with autism. All are parents of a child on the spectrum. All see the *Rowley* decision as a turning point. All are patriotic, politically active, intelligent, and well-credentialed professionals. All are tireless advocates, but the similarities end there. In Dicker's view, advocacy for legislative recognition that autism is an illness that requires health insurance coverage is a dramatic threat to special education as we know it and has far-reaching implications in the upcoming reauthorization of Public Law 94-142's successor, the Individuals with Disabilities Education Act.

Dicker stated, "I think you can make IDEA work for you, and I think the medical model, the cure model, is a pipe dream. I don't think it exists, and I think parents end up being deceived. I am not sure ABA works all that well with children over 5. I agree that it works well with young children, but I am not sure it works well with 15-year-olds except in the most severe children. The autism world is very focused on the most severe, but the autism world is composed of a very small percentage of people who are the most severe; the majority of people have mild or moderate disabilities and need all kinds of modifications and help, but I am not sure they need separate schools with an ABA model and that is based on my experience as a parent as well as an advocate."

Dicker continued, "I have real problems with the autism community seeing itself separate from the disability and special education community. What worries me about the medical model is that it is a disease model, and the disease model lends itself to not have a disability framework. The insurance laws passed in 44 states, for the most part, only deal with people with autism. That says a lot about where this community is. It says that this community thinks it is somehow different from the kid with cerebral palsy. It's different from the kids with intellectual disabilities. It's different from the kid with epilepsy" (Sheryl Dicker, personal communication, July 31, 2015).

"This is not a zero-sum game," said attorney Daniel Unumb. "We are not simply out to carve an area that benefits just us. I don't see it as something that should lead to Balkanization. I hope it will lead to change in IDEA, to a better and a more substantive view of what a meaningful education is and what the obligation of the state is with respect to kids with disabilities, just as there have been with typical kids. There is a far greater recognition that education is not simply about setting up a program; it's about an outcome. It is moving to an outcome determination of how we are doing. That is the big thing in education for typical kids; it needs to be a big thing for kids with disabilities" (Daniel Unumb, personal communication, July 18, 2016).

"I cannot apologize for working on legislative remedies that correct discrimination against people with autism," noted Judith Ursitti. "I am working on a specific problem that requires a specific solution. I don't intend to leave anyone out, but it really doesn't involve other parts of the disabilities community.

"Autism Speaks works on a variety of legislative matters. The Achieving a Better Life Experience Act (ABLE) was signed into law in late 2014. It's a disabilities savings vehicle. I worked with a broad swath of the disabilities community on ABLE. Now we have to pass legislation in all 50 states to create the accounts so people can save. We're working with the Down Syndrome Society, United Cerebral Palsy, ARC, the Autism Society, and others. ABLE is a much broader issue."

Ursitti continued, "When I first spoke to my case manager when my son was diagnosed, we were going through and talking about coverage for his different appointments. He had so many needs that the insurance company provided me with a case manager. Then I started talking very openly about his autism diagnosis and the case manager said, 'Stop right there.' She said, 'I didn't hear that.' I responded, 'I'm not ashamed that my son has autism.' At that time I was not aware that our policy excluded autism completely. The case manager said, 'No, no, no stop yourself right there. Rewind. We're not talking about autism.' So, the work I do today is not in competition with other disabilities groups; it's about getting meaningful help to everyone.

"Access to services shouldn't depend on your bank balance or your zip code, but it does. Although it's changed a bit during the last 10 years, we still have a lot of work to do so families in Oklahoma can have services just like families in Massachusetts. If the services are not exactly the same, they should at least be in the ballpark, so a kid in Oklahoma can have a fighting chance to speak, to point, to have a job or a relationship. That little kid deserves that chance" (Judith Ursitti, personal communication, August 6, 2015).

But despite the concerns of Dicker and others, for all practical purposes, the effort to recast autism in a medical model is a fait accompli. Forty plus states have autism insurance laws. Insurance companies have set up medical codes and are paying for services, and there is a dramatic increase in the number of individuals becoming Board Certified Behavior Analysts—all of this happening with public education unengaged.

Chapter Four

Autism, the Catalyst for Change

You are going to see a parent-led revolution saying special education is broken. Autism Speaks is simply the first group.

—Sonja Kerr

Even though autism numbers are increasing significantly every year, autism is still a small percentage of the whole special education population.

—Janna Lilly

According to the Centers for Disease Control and Prevention (CDC), 1 in 68 children has autism spectrum disorder (Centers for Disease Control and Prevention 2014, 6). This figure is just short of 1.5 percent. When extrapolated to the public and private K–12 school enrollment of 56 million children, the number totals 840,000. When accounting for approximately 20 million children birth to 5 years old, another 300,000 more land on the spectrum. Thus, it is estimated that more than 1 million infants, children, and adolescents have autism spectrum disorder in the United States.

The National Center for Education Statistics (2015) notes that for the 2012–2013 school year, the most recent year for which data is available, 8 percent of the 6.4 million, or 512,000, children in special education had autism, making it the fourth most prevalent disability. Behind autism in terms of prevalence were intellectual disability at 7 percent, developmental delay at 6 percent, and emotional disturbance, also at 6 percent. Special education students likewise included those with learning disabilities, language or speech impairments, and other health impairments at 35, 21, and 12 percent of the special education population respectively.

In 2013, a study presented at the Pediatric Academic Societies annual meeting stated that more children today are diagnosed with a disability than a decade ago, especially in higher-income families. "The largest increase was seen among children living in households with incomes at or above 300 percent of the federal poverty level" (Kemp 2013). According to the study's lead author, Amy J. Houtrow, MD, PhD, Chief, Division of Pediatric Rehabilitation Medicine at Children's Hospital of Pittsburgh of University of Pittsburgh Center, "The survey did not break out autism, but we suspect that some of the increase in neurodevelopmental disabilities is due to the rising incidence or recognition of autism spectrum disorder" (Kemp 2013). Houtrow and her colleagues examined disabilities alongside sociodemographic factors and are worried "that those living in poverty may be having problems with being diagnosed and getting services" (Kemp 2013).

Issues of access, of course, are widespread and appear across the board. Sherzod Abdukadirov, a regulations researcher at the Mercatus Center at George Mason University, commented, "One of the biggest drawbacks of the regulatory process is the fact that it's so complex and that it takes so much time and effort in order to participate that it essentially filters out all the voices that are less well-off. The most vulnerable really don't have as much representation in the process as the ones who are better off. If there are differences between more educated, better-off parents and less educated, less well-off parents, the better-off parents will prevail. That is one of those unintended consequences of regulation. It happens all across politics; it happens across education" (Sherzod Abdukadirov, personal communication, July 13, 2015).

Vanderbilt's Douglas Fuchs, with decades of special education policy research to his credit, noted, "I find it interesting how advocates of children and youth with autism have organized into such an effective force to promote laws at the state level, to create funding mechanisms, and to support a tremendous amount of research on autism spectrum disorder. I think that part of the differential activity that explains the greater legal activity with respect to autism is the unbelievably strong advocacy on its behalf" (Douglas Fuchs, personal communication, July 16, 2015).

With a long history of service to the disabilities community at the local, state, and federal levels, attorney Sheryl Dicker observed an event in the early 1990s that she views as a possible turning point in the way in which advocacy is conducted. "It seems like autism is striking more upper-class people and there is a sense of a cause, of a cure. There has been a huge proliferation of medical charities in the last 20 years, like those aiming to cure breast cancer, for example. Maybe it's the HIV/AIDS advocacy model, which was very contentious, that is being replicated."

Dicker explained, "I was with Bill Clinton in 1992 when HIV/AIDS activists attacked him physically. They *physically* attacked Bill Clinton when he was running for president. The HIV/AIDS community found a treatment and was very successful. And if you ask the HIV/AIDS community why they were so successful, they will tell you it was because they were so contentious. So, when a new disorder comes up, people feel like that is *the* model rather than a model of conciliation, which was the model of the early '70s—we're going to fight for everything, but we're going to fight with a smile. Physically touching Bill Clinton in 1992 would have been unheard of in 1972. You would never have done that to a superintendent or a state director of education. You would not have gone up to them, got in their face, and physically threatened them. But that is what the HIV/AIDS community did, and it worked. So, I wonder if that is the model we are now using" (Sheryl Dicker, personal communication, July 31, 2015).

The date that advocacy became more contentious has an even earlier starting point for John Pitney, Claremont McKenna College Professor of Politics, who considers the March 1988 protests at Gallaudet University in support of having a deaf president as the birth of aggressive self-determination and empowerment among advocacy groups. "The deaf advocacy movement directly and explicitly modeled itself on the African American Civil Rights Movement, and a lot of subsequent disability activists have directly and explicitly modeled themselves on deaf advocacy" (John Pitney, personal communication, July 13, 2016).

IMPATIENCE PAYS

In an era of instant communication, waiting is a lost art, and patience and civility are endangered traits. America's 21st-century political discourse is polarizing, and compromise is viewed as shameful. The social and political context of the autism crisis framed it to explode, to run rampant, and to quickly outpace the health and educational structures of the day.

Advocacy for populations with special needs is nothing new. The National Federation of the Blind began in 1940. The National Association for Retarded Citizens, now The Arc, was founded in 1950. The Learning Disabilities Association of America was established in 1964 and the Autism

Society formed one year later. These organizations, along with many others, have fought for improvements in services and opportunities for their respective groups for more than half a century, and, as Sheryl Dicker noted, they have fought with a smile. Autism Speaks emerged in 2004, and, while not physically contentious, the organization has been extremely successful and has changed the face of advocacy.

The success of Autism Speaks may be attributed to two factors. First, its founders, Bob and Suzanne Wright, while motivated by a grandson's autism diagnosis, operated at the highest levels of the mass communication industry in the United States; Bob was the former chairman and CEO of NBC. Second, Autism Speaks was born at the same time as social media and related technologies. This is not to say that other, longer-established advocacy groups did not adopt social media. These organizations, however, had built bureaucracies throughout the decades and operated at a pace and within a social fabric that characterized the second half of the 20th century. In contrast, Autism Speaks was unfettered by decades of bureaucratic weight. It was new, fresh, and embraced the technologies and organizational structures of a well-funded business start-up.

"Autism Speaks is the world's leading autism science and advocacy organization," noted C. J. Volpe, Chief of Media Strategy for Autism Speaks. "Our mission is to enhance the lives of those affected by autism across their lifespan, to fund innovative research that will lead to personalized treatments and supports for people with autism, and to advocate for the needs of people with autism on the state and federal levels. Autism Speaks cofounders Bob and Suzanne Wright's commitment; their ability to rally people within their personal and professional network around our cause; and the efforts of our board members, staff, and volunteers helped us emerge as the leading voice in the autism advocacy community on the national and international stage.

"It's fascinating how we've been successful in utilizing social media, because our pages have evolved into forums for people in the autism community to connect with each other and share their own voices. That is why we've grown exponentially on Facebook and Twitter. Those platforms provide not only an opportunity for people around the world to communicate with us but also a chance for them to communicate with each other. We were early social media adopters, and it plays a significant role in our communications. It is the way the world is changing."

Volpe continued, "In terms of raising awareness, Autism Speaks has been a business disruptor. With the emergence of new media, we were able to utilize online platforms, in addition to traditional communications, to amplify the voice of our community and make autism a household word. As such, being a business disruptor has been one of our biggest successes. Bob and Suzanne Wright's vision was to raise global awareness and educate people about autism. Educate people first, and then leverage that awareness to get legislation passed, get the research dollars that our community needs, and build up the network of service providers across the lifespan, but people have to know about autism first" (C. J. Volpe, personal communication, June 28, 2016).

Scott Badesch has spent more than 40 years in the social services field, the last five as president and CEO of the Autism Society. "I have seen significant changes with the onset of the internet, from website marketing to social media. Most disabilities organizations were set up by parents. They had a collective need to build a group home, establish a day program, or create employment programs for their kids because no one else was doing it. Public schools were legally allowed to discriminate. But as organizations developed and as technology increased, things grew more complex and beyond what could be decided at a kitchen table.

"Advocacy has changed," noted Badesch. "There are more players. You are competing within disability services, you are competing within human services, and you are competing in the wide spectrum of autism regarding such issues as money going to research versus money going to services. I was 12 years old when the Autism Society was established. But the reality is that Autism Speaks put autism on the map and has kept it on the front burner. So, if schools are dealing with more autism due process cases because parents who have children with autism turn to Autism Speaks or the Autism Society for advice, that is the school's problem because it means that the school is not adhering to the law.

"The Autism Society works well with Autism Speaks at the national level. We have our differences in certain areas, but that doesn't stop us from working together," Badesch explained. "Autism Speaks has done a good job of significantly increasing awareness of autism, and I commend the Wrights for their role in advancing the awareness of autism to where it is today. Our difference with Autism Speaks rests in that the Autism Society is focused on advancing the quality of life for all with an autism diagnosis each and every day in measurable ways based on quality of life indicators. We want to be with a person throughout his or her life by being their 'friend in caring.'

"I think what Autism Speaks has done, which is its right to do, is attempt to set the agenda on autism to focus on cause and cure. When one dominant organization owns the media message, the citizens who hear that message only receive one perspective on autism. The Autism Society is about helping the 3 million people in this country who have autism secure the opportunities that you and I take for granted. Knowing the cause of autism may be good, but having help and support and not having to wait five years for services is better."

Badesch continued, "Autism Speaks' strategic approach reflects Bob Wright's relationships with NBC and the broadcast and print media. Autism Speaks has focused a lot of national media attention on autism. This is great in one respect because it helps people know more about it, but if people are viewing autism in a way that is not in line with the way our organization wants autism to be viewed, it becomes a problem.

"Autism Speaks benefits from the history of the Autism Society, and the Autism Society benefits from the history of other groups that have advocated for their constituencies to gain access to the American Dream. That includes African American, Hispanic, and women's rights groups. The Autism Society benefited from them all, but the Autism Society is different from Autism Speaks. It does not mean that they are bad; it means that we look at things differently. The Autism Society is increasingly concerned about the infighting that can occur in the autism community. We respect differences, but we want the discussions to be respectful and solution oriented."

Badesch explained, "For instance, the Autism Society supports insurance mandates. However, we are concerned that government has to realize, due to lack of providers, services covered by mandated insurance such as ABA are not always available in low income and rural areas. Accordingly, we don't want government to view mandated insurance coverage as helping if services are not accessible. We don't wish to see government remove its responsibility for helping all individuals with a developmental disability.

"A lot of health providers do not take Medicaid. Yes, the President ordered that autism be included in Medicaid, but we have a Medicaid crisis. When there are no doctors or therapists in an area who take Medicaid or there are long waiting lists for an appointment for those who do, children will not be helped. We are offering a benefit that doesn't exist."

Badesch continued, "Further, the Autism Society has a strong position that we will not do anything to help autism at the expense of another disability group. So, if we are putting this on the back of the insurance companies, why not put all disabilities in there. It pulls our society away from dealing with the bigger issue: namely, what is the most important use of government money? So we give government an out. We don't see money going to early intervention, but we see government giving money to subsidize sports stadiums" (Scott Badesch, personal communication, February 10, 2016).

THE POWER OF BUSINESS DISRUPTORS

In many ways Autism Speaks is a business disruptor whose innovations revolutionized the landscape, just as Airbnb disrupts the hotel industry or Uber challenges taxi services. Patrick McLaughlin at the Mercatus Center at George Mason University understands how business disruptors challenge existing regulations. "A mayor is in a tough situation with regard to a disruptive company like Uber. If the mayor accepts Uber as a disruptive company competing with taxicab drivers, it is certainly the case that some taxicab drivers will lose their jobs or have to change jobs or perhaps accept a lower salary. But on the other hand, what's the alternative? You can try to keep Uber out and keep the regulations that are in place, and that is exactly what a special interest group, the taxi drivers in this case, wants to happen. But the consequences of keeping Uber out of a city, in my opinion, will be much worse than having the taxi drivers face a disruption in their industry. And the Uber battle is exactly the same kind of battle that we've fought thousands of times, in a much less public view, over special education" (Patrick McLaughlin, personal communication, August 7, 2015).

As a disruptor, Autism Speaks has moved further and faster than its older peers. It put autism on the front page, an impressive feat for the fourth most prevalent handicapping condition served by public special education. That has been the power of Autism Speaks, a power aided by its founding and coming of age alongside social media. Between 2002 and 2010 the prevalence of autism rose from 1 in 150 8-year-olds to 1 in 68. During this same time span, the following social media and technologies emerged: LinkedIn (2003), Facebook (2004), Flickr (2004), YouTube (2005), Twitter (2006), iPhone (2007), Tumblr (2007), Instagram (2010), and Pinterest (2010).

There is no causation or correlation between the frequency of autism and social media developments, but as the CDC continued to find an increase in the frequency of autism through research, Autism Speaks harnessed the power of traditional media and social media to keep autism in the news.

Julia Freeland Fisher is the director of the Clayton Christensen Institute, a think tank dedicated to improving the world through disruptive innovation with a focus on health care and education. Freeland Fisher uses a three-prong test to determine if a business practice is "disruptive." She looks at target consumers and those not getting a lot of attention at the low end of a market, she considers if the practice does not face head-to-head competition, and she also looks at if the business has a technological core that allows for scale. In adapting that test to Autism Speaks, Freeland Fisher is cautious because measuring the customer base and success milestones of an advocacy group is quite different from measuring those same things for a business.

Freeland Fisher noted, "You want to be really sharp when you make a claim about disruption and that means defining disruption as relative to what. For example, a lot of people will say online learning is disruptive relative to school. It turns out that it's not. It's actually just disruptive to teacher-led instruction. It sounds like Autism Speaks could be potentially disruptive relative to traditional nonprofit-led autism campaign work because it took a topic that few people were talking about and leveraged social media to gain significant attention."

Freeland Fisher continued, "You're really dealing in ideas here—ideas that then lead to policies that then lead to where the dollars land. In that market, Autism Speaks has been able to disproportionately distribute ideas in a manner that basically gains a stronger foothold than other advocacy groups, and that could be disruptive. It sounds to me like the potential ingredient for disruption in the Autism Speaks case is the proliferation of ideas. There was a subset of students to whom we weren't necessarily paying attention, and then someone like Bob Wright with real media savvy and good business instincts came in and really upended the establishment.

"Twenty years ago nobody was talking about autism, but there was actually a disproportionately high incidence of it relative to how many people were talking about it. Bob Wright tapped into that and found new distribution channels—media and social media. And that sounds like what Autism Speaks has managed to do. I think we would call those disruptive distribution channels relative to traditional distribution channels for advocacy" (Julia Freeland Fisher, personal communication, February 29, 2016).

As a seasoned political trainer and political consultant, Joe Fuld knows how to bring attention to an idea or a cause. He is the founder of The Campaign Workshop, a Democratic, political consulting firm in Washington, D.C., and has produced award-winning campaigns for dozens of groups including the American Cancer Society Action Network, the California Nurses Association, Defenders of Wildlife, and the Gay and Lesbian Victory Fund. Fuld is also on the Board of the International Dyslexia Association.

Fuld noted, "Advocacy is about story and it's also about engagement. Autism Speaks has been good about engaging people in their story. Today everyone either has some personal connection with autism or knows someone who has autism. People understand the effect autism has on a family and want people with autism to live a fulfilling life. At the same time it's the fear of any parent—could my child have autism?—that is also a message. Autism Speaks has been able to get those separate stories out there in a very powerful manner.

"Whether it's in the environmental movement, or women's rights, or disabilities rights, organizations leapfrog over each other if they have a better way or a clearer way of talking about something. For example, the Women's Campaign Fund was around decades before EMILY's List came on the scene, but most people don't even know the Women's Campaign Fund anymore."

Fuld explained, "Advocacy is about getting laws passed to help people. You can go down the line on issues—finding a room for a mom to breastfeed, or providing a student with extra time to take a test. Government is there to assure people of their social and civil rights and should be ready to help whether the issue is autism, dyslexia, or learning differences. It's the job of elected officials to sort through legislation and find ways that make life better for everyone" (Joe Fuld, personal communication, March 22, 2016).

Ben Shifrin also serves on the Board of the International Dyslexia Association as its vice president as well as the Headmaster of the Jemicy School in Owings Mills, Maryland. He is unapologetic in his advocacy for those with dyslexia. "I believe dyslexia organizations are following the Autism Speaks model. What this will do is allow students who have been denied services to get the services they need. Too many times what tends to happen is that public schools do not recognize the diagnosis of dyslexia. We're really missing the boat. Many dyslexics are extremely bright. So what you'll find sometimes is that they are on grade level when they should be above grade level, and the thing holding them back is their processing speed and working memory."

Shifrin continued, "We're not serving these kids, and we're hurting society in general because these students tend to be the most out-of-the-box thinkers. By recognizing dyslexia as a form of disability that requires services, not only are we going to see kids identified and really supported, if it's done correctly, we're also going to improve reading instruction across the curriculum for every child. At present, having a diagnosis of dyslexia does not even secure Section 504 services. School districts refuse to recognize it for whatever reason. By having the diagnosis, it will force schools to do screenings of children at risk for reading problems.

"Many of the legislators are afraid of the money implications of dyslexia legislation," noted Shifrin. "I don't believe it will cost any more money to put through dyslexia education. In fact, if we utilize our reading instruction money more effectively, we can take care of the dyslexia population. But every time that dyslexia legislation comes up in Maryland, legislators are fearful to add one more category. They wonder what it is going to cost the school districts, and the school districts are afraid because of the lawsuits and the IEPs that will come out of this. I think those opposing the legislation are doing so out of fear. They are not looking at it in a rational way. It's not just the child with dyslexia that's going to benefit, every child is going to benefit" (Ben Shifrin, personal communication, March 8, 2016). Due to the efforts of Decoding Dyslexia Maryland and the International Dyslexia Association, Maryland has since passed legislation recognizing dyslexia as a learning disability.

Almost every state has considered dyslexia legislation in recent years, and more than half of them have passed laws addressing such measures as early screening and creating greater access to interventions in public schools and communities. Decoding Dyslexia is the primary group behind dyslexia legislation. It is a grassroots parents' movement concerned about limited access to educational interventions for students with dyslexia. Like Autism Speaks, it bypasses frustration with public education and seeks state and federal legislative relief.

If Autism Speaks is the tip of the iceberg, then Decoding Dyslexia and the International Dyslexia Association, the Learning Disabilities Association of America, and a myriad of other organizations are waiting just below the surface to rip a jagged hole in a special education process and a federal law that places procedures over people and is unequipped to keep up with the speed of research in neurosciences and the attendant benefits for students with autism and other disabilities.

Claremont McKenna's John Pitney noted, "As the years go by, we are going to have more and more people who have grown up with either a diagnosis or educational determination of autism, and so the ranks of self-advocates will grow. That's going to change the politics. I think groups are going to look at the experience of Autism Speaks and step up their advocacy for other disability conditions. Where this ends, I don't know. But I think the next IDEA round is going to feature far more intense lobbying than we saw in 2004" (John Pitney, personal communication, July 13, 2016).

THE TRAIN HAS LEFT THE STATION

Autism Speaks is in the locomotive that now pulls a train of more than 40 states that have passed autism legislation. Autism Speaks has changed the nature of advocacy for those with disabilities by changing the nature of advocacy for those with autism. The speed and focus of the changes have left some cheering, some scratching their heads, and others upset.

Janna Lilly is the Director of Governmental Relations for the Texas Council of Administrators of Special Education (TCASE) and a former director of special education at Austin Independent School District. "There is a lot of policy discussion and activity around autism, which is interesting because autism is only one of the disability categories that we serve. It is not unusual to hear a practitioner say, 'Well yeah, my kids with autism have some significant needs, but so do my kids with visual impairments, my kids with other health impairments, and my kids with emotional disturbance. Where's the attention that they need?'"

Lilly continued, "Even though autism numbers are increasing significantly every year, autism is still a small percentage of the whole special education population. About half of the students in special education have a learning disability. So where is the voice for the child with a hearing impairment, a visual impairment, other health impairment, with emotional disturbance, or an intellectual disability?" (Janna Lilly, personal communication, August 12, 2015).

Sheryl Dicker shares Lilly's concern. "In New York City they estimate that half of the due process hearings involve autism. If you look at the caseload, autism makes up the majority of cases throughout the last 5 to 10 years. It's overwhelming. The number of children with autism is growing, but it's still not the number one disability. I have to blame the autism advocacy world, particularly Autism Speaks, for encouraging parents to make demands that I think are totally unfounded" (Sheryl Dicker, personal communication, July 31, 2015).

As Dicker's comment demonstrates, and as Autism Society's Scott Badesch noted, there is a great deal of discord within the autism community. There are disagreements on various treatment approaches, whether autism is treatable or curable, whether money should be spent on research or services, whether autism insurance coverage is the right way to go, and whether those with autism should be accepted just as they are with no or perhaps minor interventions. Directly in the middle of this discord is public education and IDEA. And just as Autism Speaks is proving to be some sort of business disruptor for advocacy groups, autism is proving to be a disruptor for the status quo of special education.

Attorney Nina Gupta sees the discord in her defense of school districts. "When you look at IDEA, it hasn't changed substantively, but case law has changed significantly when it comes to kids with autism. The two bedrock principles of IDEA are that it guarantees a basic floor of opportunity and that the methodology is within the sound discretion of the school district; IDEA does not guarantee outcomes. Those assumptions are not necessarily the case when you're dealing with kids with autism. There have been cases that specifically ordered very intensive services because, while what the school district was offering moved the student further along and provided that basic floor of opportunity, the potential of the child was much greater, so the court ordered a greater amount of service."

Gupta explained, "This type of court activism seems to be specific to autism cases. I have rarely seen that kind of analysis in an EBD case or an OHI case. Autism is really where the action is as far as litigation goes. This may be a product of the simple fact that judges are people, too, and they hear what's out in the social milieu; autism is very top of mind for a lot of people. I don't know any person at this point who doesn't know someone who's been affected by a family member with autism.

"Courts are ahead of the law or ahead of legislation when it comes to best practices for autism. There is a real melding of what has traditionally been seen as an educational model and what has been seen as a medical model. It is not necessarily just about providing educational services, which is what school districts are built for; it is essentially about curing autism without saying we're asking a school to cure autism."

Gupta continued, "The intent of Public Law 94-142 was to open up the schoolhouse doors, to bring disabled children into every part of civic life, but there has been extensive mission creep for public education. You see this happening, for example, with schools opening health centers. Traditionally, I don't think anyone had envisioned schools as health care providers, but schools are being called to do that now. I don't think anyone had envisioned schools to be community centers or to offer aftercare programs, but so many schools are doing that now as well because that's what their communities really need. But the more schools are asked to do and the further they get from their core competencies, the less able they are to do anything well, including their core competencies.

"When we're talking about a medical model, we are talking about best outcomes, about eliminating the problem, eliminating the effects of autism. When we're talking about an educational model, we are talking about preparing children so they are ready to learn. That is a much narrower set of responsibilities than the medical model.

"The more broadly a state chooses to define what education means, the easier the blurring of educational and medical models becomes," noted Gupta. "There are some states that define education as reading, writing, and arithmetic, but most states now define education as academic success, social success, emotional health, and behavioral health. In a perfect world we want every child to reach their potential, but in the spirit of *Rowley*, a school district's obligation is to make sure that a child is ready to receive the benefit of a school experience and to do the things that schools ask kids to do" (Nina Gupta, personal communication, June 22, 2015).

Special education attorney Sonja Kerr believes that autism insurance laws will not by themselves solve the problems and feels that what is happening with autism is just the beginning of the unbundling of special education. "What we are starting to see now in states that have adopted separate legislation for kids with autism or the other burgeoning part—states that have adopted legislation for kids with dyslexia—is the same non-implementation, the same kinds of fights. I don't think the issue is going to be solved by state law mandates. The schools are going to do less. That is certainly already what they are trying to do. Schools in states where there is a state insurance mandate are now telling the parents of kids with autism, 'Go talk to your insurance company.' So, the burden will just be shifted to the parents."

Kerr continued, "If all the insurance companies comply and do what they're supposed to do, that will be terrific. But now we are carving out another cottage industry of representing parents against the private insurers. Is it fun to have to represent parents in due process hearings? No. But I am not sure that it would be any better to go after insurance companies. I have done some of those cases. It is pretty intimidating to go after Blue Cross Blue

Shield, which has so many lawyers they can't even count them. But from my experience in Minnesota, when the insurance mandate went in, the schools reduced their willingness to pay.

"I have represented kids with all kinds of disabilities," noted Kerr. "I have represented kids with spina bifida, kids who are deaf, kids with intellectual disabilities, kids with dyslexia, and kids with autism. To me it is an issue of a parent's gut feeling of what is not working. Most parents are good parents and know when something is not working for their kid.

"You have a strong core of parents of kids with autism who are looking at what schools are offering or not offering and saying, 'That isn't going to work for my kid.' Autism Speaks has done a good job of giving people information," explained Kerr. "It probably is the best advocacy organization in terms of getting people right out the door. The minute your child receives an autism diagnosis or an autism diagnosis is suspected, you can click on the Autism Speaks website and get a free packet all about ABA delivered by FedEx. Nobody else is doing that.

"However, I think the parents of children with dyslexia are not that far behind. There is a grassroots push with Decoding Dyslexia. Those parents are saying, 'You know what? Wait a minute. We have a bunch of kids with dyslexia and learning disabilities, and they need stuff, too.' Those groups together, the autism parents and the dyslexia parents, are an interesting thing. It should tell special education administrators and the U.S. Department of Education what I have been saying and what other people have been saying, which is, 'You have a broken system.'"

Kerr continued, "If two of the largest groups, and they are not the only groups, but if two of the largest groups are saying that your programs are not working, and they are not just rejecting them in favor of nothing, but rejecting them in favor of something that does work, whether it's Orton-Gillingham tutoring or private school or autism ABA programming, you have a broken system. That speaks volumes.

"I went to the International Dyslexia Association conference a few years ago, and they had a session where parents could sit down with professionals and just talk. The most common statement from parents of kids with dyslexia was much more frightening than the questions about ABA and kids with autism," noted Kerr. "The question from dyslexia parents was, 'Why should I even put my kid in special education? My kid has been in special education—or my neighbor's kid has been in special education—for five years and still can't read.' That is much scarier because of the volume, because the number of kids with dyslexia makes the autism group look tiny in comparison.

"The dyslexia group is much larger in size. They are just getting started a little later than the autism group. When you see those groups really start rejecting special education, as they are starting to do, and you see those groups join with the other advocacy groups with really high numbers of kids, like kids with mental health issues, then you are going to see a parent-led revolution saying special education is broken. Autism Speaks is simply the first group. But I think that Decoding Dyslexia families are right next to them, and other groups are not that far behind. They're all saying the same thing. 'Wait a minute. I went to this school, they told me they would help my kid, they told me they would provide my kid with something that would work, and they're not delivering.'"

Kerr continued, "Special education settlements are costing school districts a fortune because school districts are not looking at the reality of programs that work for children. Unless a district has students with autism in well-validated, scientifically proven, peer-reviewed research programs that produce results, the districts are going to lose those cases. The wise districts are hiring people who are truly trained in ABA and who know how to provide ABA in sufficient numbers, how to actually provide programs. The foolish districts are trying to buck it and say, 'You know, we can provide less than that. See you in court.'

"This is not unique to autism. I had a case a year and a half ago, and the hearing officer totally hammered the district on a young man with dyslexia and said, 'This kid needs Orton-Gillingham immediately.' So I think that it's not so much autism as a frustration on the part of hearing officers. The frustration is when they are presented with clear evidence that there are programs that will educate a child, and the hearing officers feel like the school districts are not even giving it a try."

Kerr explained, "Hearing officers are hearing over and over and over again experts coming in and saying, 'You can teach kids with Asperger's. You can teach kids with dyslexia. You can teach kids with emotional disturbance. It's doable, and here's how you do it. And here is the research behind it, and it is validated.' After hearing that over and over and over, the officers become dubious of a district's claims that, 'Well, we tried a little bit of this, tried a little bit of that.' What the school districts offer just doesn't stack up against what the research recommends.

"I have argued many, many more cases where we have fought for appropriate peer-reviewed research programs in public schools than in private schools. I believe public schools should be doing these types of programs. I don't think there is anything special about these private schools being able to offer Orton-Gillingham. I think that if you put a classroom in most high schools staffed by someone who knew Orton-Gillingham, the district would be able to avoid a lot of litigation" (Sonja Kerr, personal communication, December 16, 2015).

Gerard Costa is the founding director of the Center for Autism and Early Childhood Mental Health and Professor in the Department of Early Childhood, Elementary, and Literacy Education in the College of Education and Human Services at Montclair State University. He can be counted among those concerned with the rapid evolution of autism, in part because of the failure to appreciate the complexity of the differences in human functioning it represents and because of the rigid beliefs surrounding appropriate education and intervention. "A political agenda has created a static idea of autism."

Costa continued, "A combination of inaccurate interpretation of science, propaganda, a need for us to get help for families on a larger scale, and the creation of an economic system to support it have conspired to make a behavioral approach to autism—the recommended approach by major advocacy organizations—despite the multidisciplinary and neurodevelopmental evidence that autism is not a disorder of behavior but a difference in the structure, functioning, and processing of the human brain. Professionals in no other field would be content to treat and change the symptoms without understanding their source and meaning.

"The field of autism and the nature of science, in becoming politicized and overly legislated, have been inappropriately influenced by codified approaches in law that do not allow those approaches to be adequately revised in real time or to benefit from what science is teaching us," noted Costa. "I recently met with a former high official within Autism Speaks who noted that Autism Speaks is in the midst of its own strategic planning changes. They are beginning to open up to a broader understanding of autism. But unfortunately, the form of advocacy and public education that Autism Speaks took on had the consequence of codifying rigid ways of thinking about autism.

"The evidence in ABA is iterative research. There are thousands of studies that show applied behavior analysis changes behavior. I don't think anyone would dispute that. I am an absolute believer in the principles of learning and that applied behavior analysis changes behavior. But autism is not a disorder of behavior.

"I don't think the behavior analysts read enough about the larger scientific community. Organizations like the National Autism Center have published reports on evidence-based approaches, and when the publication review panel is carefully examined, the panel is largely comprised of Board Certified Behavior Analysts," explained Costa. "The famed humanistic psychologist, Abraham Maslow, aptly noted, 'If your only tool is a hammer, everything looks like a nail.' Clearly, behaviorists will interpret behavior through that lens. The field of autism and certainly families demand more" (Gerard Costa, personal communication, March 11, 2016).

BACK TO SCHOOL

If indeed autism is a problem for our times, how should public special education programs respond? In this era of hyper-individualism, of legislation for specific handicapping conditions, of rapid and mass public action fueled by social media, can a bureaucracy as massive as public education respond in a timely manner? Brenda Van Gorder, Granite School District's Director of Special Education Preschool Services in Salt Lake City, Utah, thinks a good deal about that question. "Right now we have a disconnect between the clinical research world and the IDEA standard that public schools are held to, the standard that courts are going to use in determining if a district provides FAPE."

Van Gorder continued, "School districts cannot be locked up into a, 'Woe is me; we only get this much money from the federal government, so I am sorry but we can't do that in our district' way of thinking and practice. That attitude has to go by the wayside. There is no place for that in today's society when we have instant access to high quality interventions that work and the research to back them up.

"Why are we not using those strategies? Why are we continually going back to the same old things simply because that's what we can afford? That thinking is just not acceptable. And yet, I have to balance my budget every year. The general notion is that we better save money because we may have an expensive kid next year. We need to stop that way of thinking and use the money for the students that we have right now.

"In my current position we have services that are the intent of the law," noted Van Gorder. "It is the right thing to do and not just because it's the law.

We offer a full range of services in our preschool services program because it's the right thing to do for children. Since we offer a full range of services, our children with autism have every kind of option, from services in a general education classroom, to a self-contained classroom, to a one-on-one ABA intensive program provided by the public school.

"There is a much higher incidence of autism today than we would have ever thought possible just a decade or so ago. I think autism was either previously misdiagnosed or called other things. If not, we truly have a national crisis or phenomenon with the increase of autism. It is scary. People want to know more about it and get it fixed and make sure that it doesn't happen in their family. And if it does happen in their family, they want to know that there is help out there to make things better for their kids and grandkids."

Van Gorder continued, "People will rally around a cause, and the bigger it gets, the more organized it gets, and legislation easily follows because autism touches so many people, but some of our other disabilities have much lower incidence rates and touch fewer people. I don't know that there is going to be a group that will come forward and advocate for our young children with spina bifida on the same level that we have around autism. I just don't see that happening, even though it is just as devastating to those families who have children with spina bifida and other low incidence disabilities.

"And we hear about that concern," Van Gorder explained. "Here in Utah our legislators have asked, 'If we do this for our children with autism, what will the next group that's going to come forward need, and are we going to have separate legislation for each one of the categories? Are we going to get to a place of having categorical funding for every kind of disability?' And one of our legislators asked, 'How do we stop that?'" (Brenda Van Gorder, personal communication, October 9, 2015).

Cathy Pratt is the Director of the Indiana Resource Center for Autism at the Indiana Institute on Disability and Community and speaks for many in public special education. "I don't know whether beating up a school system is really effective. I hope that people will think about how to be part of the solution and not part of the problem. I know in our state people are feeling very beaten up, so being beaten up even more is not going to result in good outcomes for kids. I think it's all about how we pull together, whether it's ABA providers or school providers. Our responsibility is to figure out how we can get people to work together and not further silo services. How do we pull people together so we can collectively give children our best?" (Cathy Pratt, personal communication, August 7, 2015).

REFERENCES

Centers for Disease Control and Prevention. 2014. "Prevalence of Autism Spectrum Disorder among Children Aged 8 Years—Autism and Developmental Disabilities Monitoring Network, 11 Sites, United States, 2010." *Morbidity and Mortality Weekly Report* 63(2): 1–21.

Kemp, C. 2013. "Childhood Disability Rate Jumps 16 Percent over Past Decade." *AAP News*. Retrieved from http://www.aappublications.org/content/early/2013/05/05/aapnews .20130505-2 (February 17, 2016).

National Center for Education Statistics. 2015. "Children and Youth with Disabilities" (Last Updated: May 2015). Retrieved from http://nces.ed.gov/programs/coe/indicator_cgg.asp (February 17, 2016).

Chapter Five

Reality Passes Regulation

When you read the statute in and of itself, it's not bad. It's when you get to the regulations that you see it is out of control.

        —Phyllis Wolfram

I think we have to have hard conversations about not only how we spend our resources, but whether we really need to lay this at the feet of school districts.

        —Nina Gupta

As the nation edges closer to its next reauthorization of IDEA, those charged with the task look upon a landscape that has changed dramatically since 2004 and radically since 1975. In its 40 plus years of existence, IDEA has taken many forms. Historical, geographic, regulatory, and cultural factors have created great variation in the focus, quality, and importance of special education. California and Massachusetts established cultures, even before Public Law 94-142, that honor diversity and see those with disabilities as valuable members of the community. Those states also have a history of relying on science and best practices in designing law and administering programs.

Most other states rely less on clinical approaches to aspects of special education including the behavioral sciences. The perspective that children use free will to choose their behavior and that the criminal justice system may serve as the ultimate backstop is an unfortunate reality in much of the country. Special education has extreme variation in focus and quality, far more variation than found in English, mathematics, or interscholastic sports across the nation.

Public education is primarily a state function with significant local input and is strongly influenced by the federal government. The Center on Budget and Policy Priorities specified that nationwide, states contribute 46 percent to K–12 education funding, local revenue funds 45 percent, and federal revenue funds 9 percent of the overall share (Leachman, Albares, Masterson, and Wallace 2015). The report noted that at least 31 states provided less support for public schools in 2014 than in the prerecession year of 2008 and that 15 of those states have seen cuts in excess of 10 percent. The wide variation in how states fund public schools in part helps explain the wide variation in special education services, a variation that frustrates many.

"Many special educators are not taking advantage of the knowledge that we have," noted Lorri Unumb, Vice President of State Government Affairs for Autism Speaks. "I think generally good people are drawn into special education. There's no nefarious intent here, but there is this kind of pervasive inertia" (Lorri Unumb, personal communication, July 18, 2016).

That pervasive inertia that Unumb sees was evident in July 2016 when the U.S. Department of Education released its mandated annual review of IDEA stating that only 24 states qualified as meeting the requirements of the federal law and that 26 states needed assistance or intervention in implementing the law. Even four decades into the law, a majority of states still fail to implement IDEA to the satisfaction of the U.S. Department of Education.

Thomas Higbee, a professor of special education and rehabilitation at Utah State University, summed up the patchwork nature of the landscape of American special education. "The way IDEA is interpreted and applied state to state and place to place is broad and varied and depends on the circumstance, finances, and the culture of the place. Each district still approaches special education in an individual way."

Higbee continued, "Parents today are much more aware of the range of services available and of the general support from the public schools for those kinds of specialized services. Unlike other kinds of disability categories, there has emerged a class of specialized services that have been shown to be effective for kids on the autism spectrum. That's certainly had an impact on the way public education addresses the needs of students on the autism spectrum, and that varies from district to district and state to state" (Thomas Higbee, personal communication, August 11, 2015).

South Dakota special education director Michelle Powers speaks for many special education leaders when she addressed the issue of "fully funded." "We have never been fully funded. We don't even really know what fully funded means in actual dollars. It's just a formula phrase.

"When the stimulus dollars came out from the Obama Administration, I probably got twice the allocation that I typically do. But there were so many federal nuances to all of it because of maintenance efforts and other restrictions with what you could and couldn't do with the dollars; it was like seeing the Holy Grail and you couldn't do anything with it. But for one brief moment, you knew what the potential of almost full funding felt like."

Powers continued, "Government turns on itself all the time. Here's the cure. Here's the fix. Here's this. Here's that. Gerald Ford, who didn't want to sign it, put Public Law 94-142 into place. Ford knew it was going to cost a lot of money, but he did sign it, and it is the law, and it will not go away. But it's like so many things in our government. It doesn't rise to the level of importance to actually have somebody say, 'Our word is our bond, and we're going to do what we said we would do'" (Michelle Powers, personal communication, June 10, 2016).

As Executive Director of Special Programs for the Springfield, Missouri, Public Schools, Phyllis Wolfram oversees special education, gifted education, Section 504, Title I, early childhood, and English language learner programs. She is also the Policy and Legislation Chair of the Council of Administrators of Special Education (CASE), an affiliate of the Council for Exceptional Children. "We know that IDEA is well overdue for reauthorization," Wolfram noted. "I have had the opportunity to pull a couple of different committees together from across the United States to listen to special education directors talk about reauthorization of IDEA and what needs to be changed. When you read the statute in and of itself, it's not bad. It's when you get to the regulations that you see it is out of control. It is so highly regulated, so compliance driven."

Wolfram explained, "The regulations keep stacking and stacking and stacking and they need a major revision. Regulation is the box in which we are stuck. We need to go outside the box and think more about real services for students and what that should look like in our communities. I do not think it is evolving to a public education versus medical model. It is the whole environment of the child, the home setting coupled with public education and the home setting coupled with the medical model. If the medical model and the educational model could come together, we would see more successes for those kids who are less privileged in their home environment" (Phyllis Wolfram, personal communication, July 22, 2015).

The bridging of the medical and educational models that Wolfram seeks has been under development for a number of years in Indiana. Cathy Pratt, the Director of the Indiana Resource Center for Autism, collaborates with Stephan Viehweg, a research professor in the Riley Child Development Center at the Indiana University School of Medicine. Pratt explained that, "Steve and I have been involved in an initiative in the state to look at how we can bring ABA programs and schools closer together to minimize some of the tension that's occurring between the two." Viehweg added, "Cathy and I have been involved in a collaborative effort for a number of years to try and keep pulling people together to work out these issues."

"Indiana was the first state to have an insurance mandate, and it's the gold standard of insurance mandates," stated Pratt. "Indiana has been successful legislatively because we've actually worked in collaboration. What we have found is that when we don't, or when we splinter off and do not come together, we hurt ourselves legislatively. As a state, we have worked hard on working together and on not working against each other. We use a model of collective impact; it's a shared leadership design."

Pratt explained, "We pulled an ABA workgroup together. We included people from clinics, providers, individuals at the state level, and people in a university setting doing BCBA programs and found that we were all speaking a different language. We had to get around the table and start learning each other's language. It's been interesting. One of the articles we wrote focused on what families should look for in ABA providers. Building consensus around articles and publications takes time, but because we built consensus, we're able to move our field a bit forward.

"We all saw that there was a need to respectfully sit down at the table, honor the work that everyone does, and figure out how schools and ABA centers can complement each other," noted Pratt. "So ABA centers can work on the medical and neurological aspects of autism and schools can work on the social aspects, the connections with peers, and academic standards. And we can all talk about transitioning kids to adult services. Years of research have told us that when children are educated in segregated settings, they end up in segregated settings as adults. So, we need to work together and do the very best on behalf of the child" (Cathy Pratt and Stephan Viehweg, personal communication, August 4, 2015).

The spirit of cooperation among professionals found in Indiana has yet to flourish in most other states. The superintendent of the School District of Menomonee Falls, Wisconsin, Patricia Fagan Greco, started her career as a special education teacher. She also has two daughters moving into professions focused on children with special needs; one is studying speech therapy, the other, occupational therapy, and both are completing the autism certificate in their training.

"My daughter was trained by an ABA company as an in-home line therapist," explained Fagan Greco. "Having the ability for her to understand the needs of a child from the family's perspective was life changing for her. It will make her a better therapist. It will make her a better educator. It will make her a better team member all the way around. She understands the challenges parents face every morning and what their hopes are for their child. She also understands the roles educators and therapists play to bring those hopes to reality."

Fagan Greco continued, "But I don't think there is a single college campus that actually bridges the therapy students into the workings of the education arena. From a legal standpoint, from a policy standpoint, from a funding standpoint, it's all siloed. We're absolutely trapped in politics right now—the politics of vouchers, the politics around choice. People have made the language right or wrong rather than focusing on how we may serve children better. The more we banter back and forth, the more damaging it is to actually having those deeper conversations because it builds up the walls. We're losing sight of the needs of the children" (Patricia Fagan Greco, personal communication, July 23, 2015).

As more and more children are diagnosed with autism; as special education programs and ABA programs continue, for the most part, along separate tracks; and as the remaining states pass legislation specifying health insurance coverage for children with autism, what are the prospects for a reauthorized IDEA to respond meaningfully to such a complex situation? Patrick McLaughlin, a senior research fellow in the Regulatory Studies Program at the Mercatus Center at George Mason University, specializes in regulations and the regulatory process and understands how regulation begets regulation.

"It's not just a Department of Education problem; regulation accumulates over time," McLaughlin explained. "If you took all the federal regulations that were in effect in 2014 and you tried to read them from eight to five on a full-time basis with two weeks of vacation a year, you'd be reading for about three years straight. In the 1970s when special education laws were just beginning and were being translated into regulations, the number of pages of federal regulations was less than half of what it is today.

"Regulation is a government-specific phenomenon," explained McLaughlin. "It's the nature of bureaucracies. In the private sector, such bloat is eventually punished. In the quest for profits and efficiencies, owners or stockholders revolt and private enterprises cut away the chaff. You might say that citizen voters have some corollary power to stockholders, but the difference is that effects of regulations and regulatory accumulation are well-hidden. And, speaking from experience as one who worked within a federal regulatory agency, your incentive is to be part of the teams that make new regulations."

A further complication in the reauthorization process, in McLaughlin's view, is protecting the status quo for those who make a living on the basis of existing regulations. "It's the case for every regulation; special interests form to try to keep it in place. There are always winners and losers. Typically, the winners tend to be more concentrated and the losers tend to be more dispersed" (Patrick McLaughlin, personal communication, August 7, 2015).

Sherzod Abdukadirov, also a research fellow in the Regulatory Studies Program, noted that, "When you are trying to regulate a complex phenomenon with a lot of variability across the board, you basically end up with suboptimal solutions for everybody because it has to be a single regulatory solution" (Sherzod Abdukadirov, personal communication, July 13, 2015).

The recasting of autism as a health care concern leaves in its wake other disabilities communities wondering if their participation in the shaping of the special education environment has been too conciliatory and selfless. It leaves questions about Medicaid funding for children with autism in states that have not expanded services and public school districts wondering what a handicapping condition with health care insurance behind it means for them. It has professional associations not seeing eye-to-eye on who should deliver specific services to children with autism. It places special education hearing officers and judges in positions to shape case law far ahead of the reauthorization. It leaves millions of families, particularly the poor, out of the process. And many of the nation's leaders in Washington have a different perspective from those a generation or two before.

"We no longer have Ted Kennedy, and we no longer have the people in his office who were wonderful, wonderful advocates for IDEA and special education. Jim Jeffers is gone. Tom Harkin is gone. I haven't seen other great advocates emerge. It will be an interesting conversation. And since RTI was written into IDEA, people have wondered what it's doing in IDEA when it's a general education initiative and perhaps better suited for ESEA (now

ESSA)," mused Maureen O'Leary Burness, who recently retired as a career special educator after cochairing California's Statewide Special Education Task Force (Maureen O'Leary Burness, personal communication, August 5, 2015).

New York attorney Sheryl Dicker also sees changes in the political landscape. "If you look at the states that have passed insurance equity laws, you will find that the sponsors are not your traditional sponsors of disability legislation, who typically are moderate or liberal legislators. Those sponsoring insurance equity are generally very, very conservative" (Sheryl Dicker, personal communication, July 31, 2015).

Aubrey Daniels, who switched from clinical psychology because traditional clinical therapies did not work and now uses applied behavior analysis in his organizational management consultancy, Aubrey Daniels International, related, "I remember talking to Jeb Bush when he was governor of Florida. I was telling him about a program where we were going to put a BCBA in every school and train the teachers. And Jeb said to me, 'Behavior analyst? What in the hell is a behavior analyst?' So, I knew I had some work to do" (Aubrey Daniels, personal communication, July 17, 2015).

Gina Green, the executive director of the APBA, is certain that Jeb Bush is not alone when it comes to knowing about applied behavior analysis. "I don't know if I'll live that long, but I hope to see applied behavior analysis accepted in the various areas where it can help our society. In public schools, ABA is often unknown or misunderstood, and where it is utilized in an IEP, it is part of a patchwork of services."

Green continued, "So in many school districts I've seen that have said, 'Okay, we're going to try to provide some ABA services,' and maybe they've hired a Board Certified Behavior Analyst, the kids may spend a little bit of their time during each school day being exposed to some ABA techniques. But they're still going down the hall and getting sensory integration therapy from the occupational therapist and going off to speech therapy sessions for half-an-hour or two half-hours a week, which can't begin to address their pervasive needs in the area of communication skills.

"There is often an issue with teacher contracts," noted Green. "I can't tell you how many behavior analysts I've talked to who had been hired by a school district as an ABA consultant but then were literally not allowed to train teachers and aides. That is, they were not allowed to provide them with real training by demonstrating what to do and then having them implement techniques with the behavior analyst providing feedback. That is not allowed by many contracts that say that the only people who can provide training and performance evaluations of school employees are the special education director or the principal.

"So behavior analysts don't have the control that they need, frankly, to hire and train people to implement applied behavior analysis methods in those schools. There are exceptions, but they are rare. And it's not just with regard to students with autism," explained Green. "There's a lack of a thoroughgoing commitment to using techniques that have proven effective in sound scientific studies and to hiring people who are trained and thoroughly qualified in those techniques and letting them have control of curricula and of personnel to implement them. That's politics. It's due partly, to my way of thinking, to the IDEA. And it's been this way for many, many years" (Gina Green, personal communication, July 14, 2015).

Nina Gupta, the attorney who focuses on special education law and represents dozens of school districts, noted, "The floor of services that IDEA guarantees is not what any parent wants for their child. They don't want adequate educational opportunity. No parent wants that. And I think, with autism in particular, we really have a case of mission creep for schools. The law overall has not really changed substantively in many, many, many years. And yet the law surrounding serving kids with autism has changed pretty significantly with the case law. And that's really where I think the action is when you're talking about IDEA and serving kids with autism."

Gupta noted, "I think we have to have hard conversations about not only how we spend our resources, but whether we really need to lay this at the feet of school districts. And this just gives you a foundational premise here that we are at a point where we are well beyond the competencies—forget core competencies, just competencies of a school district—and we have to think a little bit bigger to crack this nut.

"I have yet to meet an educator who doesn't want to do the best possible for every child and doesn't want to see every single child reach his or her potential. And, by golly, if it were up to them, if it were a 50-hour-a-week, year-round, one-on-one program, they'd be all for it. But the realities just don't let them do that" (Nina Gupta, personal communication, June 22, 2015).

Brenda Van Gorder, a director of special education preschool services, has built an outstanding preschool program for more than 3,000 children in Granite City, Utah, 700 of whom have IEPs. She also has three BCBAs on her staff. "The private sector and the clinical world keep pulling the public schools along and really force our hands to look at things in a different way. It's not a bad thing for us to be forced to look at things in a different way.

"That being said, we also do not have infinite amounts of money. IDEA has never been fully funded by the federal government, so there's the funding gap," explained Van Gorder. "There was never an expectation that the federal government would cover all of the expenses. States and local governments were expected to pick up the other percentage, and yet we fall short across the nation. I think it is a crisis across the nation to adequately fund what we now know works."

Van Gorder continued, "Services for children with autism are not inexpensive. But we have other kinds of disabilities where we have proven strategies that are also expensive. So, where do we get the funds at a public school level to make that happen? Do you do that on the backs of the other children with disabilities who aren't requiring those other services? It's a hard tension, and if you're in an administrative role, how do you make all of your funds stretch and do the right thing beyond *Rowley*?" (Brenda Van Gorder, personal communication, October 9, 2015).

Janna Lilly, the TCASE's Director of Governmental Relations, noted, "I think it's just a really great time to have this discussion because there is not an educator around who would not say that, if resources and funding were no object, we would want to maximize the education of every single child with and without a disability."

Lilly continued, "I think that Public Law 94-142 was some of the most basic, brilliant legislation and did some phenomenal things for our kids with disabilities; Public Law 94-142 opened the door. It gave our kids access to public schools and public education. Then along comes IDEA. I think, however, that IDEA has become out of control. We've taken the focus off of student progress. I would love to see an IDEA reauthorization, just a start over, a reignition, a Stephen Covey model—begin with the end in mind" (Janna Lilly, personal communication, August 12, 2015).

As a BCBA, Matt Briere-Saltis is hired by families in the Jacksonville, Florida, area to work with their children in public schools. "Autism is such a complex thing. It spans the medical, psychological, and educational fields. It's in the home. It's in the family. It's a big part of things that are important to the American people. It has a profound effect on families. It is not going away. It is not changing. The need to address autism is only going to grow. It is something that can't be underemphasized (Matt Briere-Saltis, personal communication, September 15, 2015).

INSTITUTIONAL BARRIERS TO CHANGE

Those who work daily with children with autism, including Powers, Gupta, Van Gorder, and Lilly, address issues such as underfunding, overregulation, and inadequate preservice training and call on schools to do something beyond their competencies. In their voices is a sense of urgency, a sense that autism is challenging special education in a way that not only has bearing on the children themselves but also on the very framework of special education.

Will special education grow, stretch, and change in keeping with the complexities of autism? Will preservice training for special education teachers demand more in-depth study of behavioral sciences and neurosciences? Will special education adopt a more medical model of maximum benefit? Will it rise, to paraphrase Powers, to a level where our government and public schools will do what they said they would do in the spirit of the law passed in 1975?

After years of working with state legislatures to pass autism insurance, Lorri Unumb prays that the questions above are answered in the affirmative. "Having a child who's severely impaired with autism is frustrating on so many levels. It impacts your family emotionally, it impacts your stability, and it impacts you financially, and there is no reason why an autism diagnosis needs to be financially devastating for a family. There is nothing the government can do about the emotional devastation, but the financial devastation can be alleviated.

"That's one reason I have spent the last 10 years working on the insurance laws—to help alleviate that piece," Unumb explained. "Portability of IEPs likewise could alleviate some of the financial devastation as well as the exhaustion and frustration. I think the problem is the patchwork that I keep referring to.

"If IDEA were fully funded and all states and all school districts were offering special education services that were even remotely similar to each other, then maybe there could be portability, but as it is now, what you get in a special education classroom in Massachusetts and what you get in a special education classroom in the Deep South do not even appear to be related. It is difficult to believe that they are considered to meet the same federal law. So the portability of IEPs is simply impractical right now for reasons that should not exist" (Lorri Unumb, personal communication, July 18, 2016).

REFERENCE

Leachman, M., Albares, N., Masterson, K., and Wallace, M. 2015. "Most States Have Cut School Funding, and Some Continue Cutting." Retrieved from http://www.cbpp.org/re-search/state-budget-and-tax/most-states-have-cut-school-funding-and-some-continue-cutting (December 21, 2015).

Chapter Six

Is There a BCBA in the House?

Behavior analysis is an independent discipline and applied behavior analysis is
an independent profession.

—James Carr

We have to be honest enough with ourselves in recognizing that the "act" of
science is not simply an academic or high-level, moral inquiry. We would be
foolish to ignore the economic motivations.

—Gerard Costa

Applied behavior analysis is not just for children with autism. Aubrey Daniels started his career in the 1960s as a clinical psychologist but was frustrated when traditional clinical therapies did not work and he did not get the results he wanted. "Fortunately, I was introduced to behavior modification, as it was called in those days. I was working in Atlanta at an institute to train mental health professionals for the state and began using behavior modification with adult patients there. I got what I'd call even today 'amazing results.' The patients responded rapidly and changed their behavior, and some behaviors had been going on for years.

"One woman had been receiving shock treatment for 26 years," noted Daniels. "She was 52 at the time, suffered from agoraphobia, and was admitted to the Georgia Mental Health Institute. After I started treatment, she was discharged in about a month. I continued to see her for a couple of months on an outpatient basis and maintained contact with her until she died at 92. She called me every year on my birthday and lived a very happy and fruitful life from 52 to 92. I began using ABA in everything I did—in shelter workshops with mildly developmentally delayed children and at a state hospital vocational rehabilitation center in North Carolina. I used ABA everywhere I went, and it worked and just kept snowballing."

Daniels continued, "Eventually I went into the business arena. I knew ABA could help in the business world, and I got a chance to apply it in North Carolina. Cannon Mills, a textile company, had one plant with almost 11,000 employees, and the turnover was just horrendous—close to 200 percent of their people within 90 days of hire. They had to hire three people to keep one on the job. It was a huge problem.

"The vice president of human resources was skeptical that ABA would work and asked me to tell him where I had been using it. I described my clinical experiences, but he was still skeptical that it would work in a business environment. It was a good thing for me that the mill had tried just about everything else and that nothing had worked. We got the job, and we cut the 90-day turnover rate in half in 90 days. That led to our working throughout the textile industry; we could not keep up with the demand.

"Many people today do not seem to get that it's about changing behavior," explained Daniels. "It doesn't matter where the behavior is; we learn from our environment. And if we learn from our environment, then it doesn't matter what your DNA is either. Whether you are working with kids with autism or a developmentally delayed child, or an adult trying to manage the affairs of the family or an owner trying to improve a personal business, applied behavior analysis has something to offer" (Aubrey Daniels, personal communication, July 17, 2015).

Aubrey Daniels's management consulting firm has used the principles of behavioral sciences to improve the workplace in more than 160 industries around the world. Daniels is a noted writer and speaker on implementing applied behavior analysis in the workplace, and he is not alone in his support of ABA as a science that has wide applicability.

Corey Robertson is a BCBA and lead co-instructor in continuing education at the Florida Institute of Technology. Robertson began his career in 1998 as an exceptional education teacher for Orange County Public Schools in Florida. He has worked as a behavior analyst in homes, schools, and community settings, and his enthusiasm for ABA is evident as noted, "I firmly believe that behavior analysts can change the world and that all behavior analysts need to think this way. It's going to take some time, and we certainly need to grow. Part of it is through good training programs and part of it is through educating consumers.

"As you increase your knowledge and awareness of applied behavior analysis, you see that it not only helps children with autism, but that it also helps a lot of other kids as well as adults. As ABA becomes popular, you get more and more people saying, 'We do ABA. We offer ABA. We're an ABA clinic. We do that.' But when people don't actually understand what they are doing, a couple of things happen. One is that children don't actually get better and two is that parents waste their time and money. In some cases, people can even get hurt. Children's lives are at stake; I firmly believe that. It comes down ultimately to the quality of care and the protection of the children."

Robertson continued, "I joke that I like to cook, but when I cook I don't call it doing 'culinary arts' because I didn't go to culinary school. I don't do culinary arts; I cook. I always tell people, 'Don't say you do ABA unless you have a credential in ABA.' A behavior analyst program at a master's level involves a lot of nitty-gritty science, natural science, and single-subject design methodology; it also includes the philosophy of radical behaviorism. The reason we have the profession of behavior analysis is because people got hurt under the guise of behavior modification. We have to ensure that the people who work with the most vulnerable populations have the appropriate training and experience to do ABA.

"It started here in Florida as a training program for folks working with individuals with disabilities through the state Medicaid program and eventually grew to other states including Pennsylvania, Texas, and Oklahoma," explained Robertson. "Then the Behavior Analyst Certification Board emerged, and now we are in this licensure phase where we are getting the teeth on a state-by-state basis to enforce and make sure that people are engaged in the standards of practice that we have established."

Today 24 states have licensure boards for BCBAs, and the number is expanding. While Robertson believes that ABA can apply to a wide array of human problems, he recently conducted an estimation of how many BCBAs are needed for America's children with autism. "The BACB practice guidelines for autism talk about focused treatment without the support of a BCaBA and put a caseload at anywhere from 10 to 15 cases. For comprehensive treatment without a BCaBA, the behavior analyst would have 6 to 12 cases, so we are talking about a range of 6 to 15 cases. For my estimation, I determined that a 10 full-time client to one BCBA ratio would be a fair approximation. With an estimated 1 million children in the U.S. with autism, we need 100,000 behavior analysts."

Robertson continued, "I also wondered how many BCBAs are needed to serve a wider population of children with disabilities. I examined the National Indicators of Well-Being that pulls data from 23 federal agencies. Among the questions parents were asked was if their children had emotional difficulties. In 2013, 5 percent of children were reported by their parents as having serious difficulties with emotions, concentration, behavior, or getting along with others, and 22 percent of those reported were getting special education services. To me, every one of those kids could benefit from a behavior analyst.

"Another 13 percent were reported as having minor difficulties, and 10 percent of those were receiving special education services. I end up with an estimated 24.4 million children who can benefit from applied behavior analysis. What does this mean? It means that we need 2.4 million behavior analysts if we account for all the children in the U.S. with autism or with emotional or behavioral issues that ABA can address.

"ABA doesn't just apply to kids with autism, and it really doesn't just apply to kids with behavior problems either," noted Robertson. "You can look at any human problem from that perspective and gain some insight. It is a wonderful science that changes lives by helping individuals learn skills and achieve their goals in life. It is a great approach to solving human problems" (Corey Robertson, personal communication, October 30, 2015).

THE CARE AND NURTURING OF A PROFESSION

As the CEO of the Behavior Analyst Certification Board, James Carr holds a key position in the professionalization of the discipline of behavior analysis. "The BACB was founded in 1998. It was the outgrowth of a state certification program for behavior analysts in Florida that had been operating since the late '70s and found its footing in the late '80s and early '90s. It was really quite successful. Florida was a state that early on had a concentration of behavior analysts in university preparation programs and behavior-analytic jobs wired into the developmental disability service system. So, there was a need early on to identify individuals with certain competencies in the discipline."

Carr explained, "In the '90s, other states that had similar needs to identify behavior analysts started contracting with Florida to use Florida's examination. These included California, Oklahoma, Texas, New York, and Pennsylvania. Dr. Jerry Shook, who initially oversaw the Florida system, realized that there was a national need for an organization to provide behavior-analytic credentials. There were no other credentials of the kind at the time. He entered into a contractual relationship with the state of Florida for the BACB to assume the oversight and maintenance of all the Florida certificants and to use examination materials in the BACB's broader efforts.

"That was the BACB, and it was founded and incorporated in 1998. During the next few years Florida phased out its system, so most Florida certificants were brought in under the new credentials, but we still actually maintain about 50 individuals who are Florida certified behavior analysts from back in the day.

"Dr. Jerry Shook, the founding CEO, had the most knowledge of regulation of the practice during the formation of a discipline where professionalization did not occur until we had a scientific basis and had some amount of technology developed," noted Carr. "Dr. Shook started communicating with behavior analysts through the peer-reviewed literature and through conferences all over the world to spread the word about the need for some sort of credential to identify individuals with minimal level competencies.

"That is what a professional credential is. It shows that an individual has met minimum education and training standards in a profession, and it provides a floor and an entry point for the profession. Then, of course, individuals acquire additional expertise and competencies in different areas."

Carr continued, "Throughout the 2000s, Dr. Shook was quite successful in growing the number of individuals pursuing certification in universities that offered courses in a certain way or a certain combination of topics to prepare individuals to apply for the credential. In 2007, Dr. Shook obtained accreditation of our two primary behavior analyst credentials, the Board Certified Behavior Analyst and the Board Certified Assistant Behavior Analyst. These accreditations were obtained from the National Commission for Certifying Agencies. This is the organization that, in North America, establishes best practices for how professional credentials should be developed and operated and maintained over time.

"Pursuing accreditation meant two things," explained Carr. "It meant that the BACB was operating according to best practices in the credentialing and professional industries, but it also gave recognition and added legitimacy to the organization to various stakeholders like legislators and funders. As societal demand for applied behavior-analytic services grew, so did a need to identify, by governments and funders, individuals who had formal training in behavior analysis. We had more individuals applying to take our examinations in the hope of becoming credentialed with the BACB. I came on as CEO in 2011. Just this month (June 2015) we have certified our 20,000th behavior analyst worldwide.

"We obtained certification for our discipline first, and then came licensure. Licensure is written into law; it has a statutory basis and regulates the practice of a profession in that state. The first states to pass a licensure bill were Nevada and Oklahoma in 2009. It was only relatively recently that some states started requiring practitioners to be licensed by the state in order to practice."

Carr noted, "The BACB had been operating for 11 years up to that point and had done the heavy lifting in terms of conducting the extensive study workgroups necessary to identify task list competencies, coursework, eligibility, and experience requirements to sit for the examination; the CEU and maintenance requirements for credentials; and the exam, which, of course, is quite an undertaking. Because all of that already existed, beginning in 2009, most states that have passed licensure laws have either written our credential or our standards into licensure requirements.

"An example of the former approach is Oklahoma," explained Carr. "To be a licensed behavior analyst in the state of Oklahoma you must submit proof to the state that you are a Board Certified Behavior Analyst in good standing with the BACB. That is your primary requirement to be licensed in the state. Those individuals are dually credentialed. They are credentialed by the state under licensure and they are credentialed by us with certification. That means we have two levels of disciplinary oversight. We take disciplinary action against certificants for misconduct, and the state does the same. That is one model of licensure."

Carr continued, "The other example is where our standards are written into the law. Some states, instead of writing in a credential, prefer to simply write in what our requirements are at the time. For example, Arizona wrote in that you must have 225 hours of graduate coursework in behavior analysis, which is coincidentally our requirement for coursework. Then you needed to have 1,500 hours of experience, which is one of our experience requirements. You had to have a master's degree, and you had to pass a national exam. We offer the only national exam, so for those states—although our credential itself is not written as the primary eligibility requirement—our requirements are broken down and written into the law. Functionally, most of those individuals are also dually credentialed.

"Behavior analysis is an independent discipline," Carr noted, "and applied behavior analysis is an independent profession. Historically, behavior analysis split off from academic psychology in the '50s. It emerged from psychology, but it did not emerge from within clinical psychology. Skinner's work occurred before there was clinical psychology, so our roots are really in developmental and experimental psychology, but we started doing things on our own—with our own journals and our own professional associations—more than half a century ago. Since then, we have evolved in parallel with the work of other professions like speech-language pathology and clinical psychology."

Carr continued, "When it comes time to regulate the practice of the applied behavior analysis profession in a state, the profession should be regulated by its own members. I think the ideal arrangement is that a state establishes an independent behavior analyst licensure board, just as there is a psychology board and a speech board and an OT board, et cetera. Of the states that offer licensure, the most common is a behavior analyst board, followed closely by behavior analysts who are regulated by psychology boards. We also find behavior analysts regulated by what we call an omnibus board that is comprised of multiple mental health professions. It is possible that at the end of this year (2015), the majority of U.S. states will have licensure. It is likely that next year we'll have another 5 to 10 states pursue it.

"It is important to distinguish the fact that the role of a professional credential—be it a professional certification in the discipline, like you have with the BACB, or at the state level through licensure—does not guarantee quality or measure quality per se. All professional credentials do is establish entry standards for the profession. Credentials demonstrate some level of minimal competence, usually through the passage of a psychometrically sound examination. The credential itself facilitates a workforce having some level of quality, but it doesn't guarantee it.

"Every profession has a starting point when the standards are lower than ideal because you can't grow a profession with a couple hundred people," explained Carr. "You have to have people who still meet minimum requirements, but the requirements are not set at the terminal goal so that you can actually get bodies in the field. Of course, a profession will not be written into any law or recognized if there is not a sufficient number of practitioners to make it seem like a legitimate enterprise. Ten years from now it will be substantially more difficult to become a BCBA than it was 10 years ago.

Again, this is a natural developmental process for a credential and for a profession as well."

Carr noted, "In the United States, there are three major organizations that support the discipline. I lead the BACB, our credentialing organization. The Association for Behavior Analysis International is our scientific society, and its mission is based on science. They do support practice and practitioners, but through scientific initiatives. The Association of Professional Behavior Analysts is a relatively young organization. It was developed primarily to deal with issues that are germane to practitioners rather than to all behavior analysts. APBA is the organization most heavily involved in legislative activities and activities that really are designed to directly support and advocate on behalf of practitioners. That is how the landscape appears to be shaping up in behavior analysis.

"From my perspective, this is a pretty good division of labor. Organizations collaborate when it is important to collaborate. When collaborative opportunities are lacking, there is respectful recognition that different actors handle different parts of the equation" (James Carr, personal communication, June 30, 2015).

BUT NOT EVERYONE IS HAPPY

New professions edge into territory held by incumbent practitioners. The medical profession looked askance at the professionalization of psychologists who then expressed concern about social workers and so on. And so it is with behavior analysts. The profession coexists with other professions and with academics who had hoped the science would have taken another path.

Founded in 1925, the American Speech-Language-Hearing Association (ASHA) is the national professional, scientific, and credentialing association for more than 186,000 members and affiliates who are audiologists; speech-language pathologists; speech, language, and hearing scientists; audiology and speech-language pathology support personnel; and students. ASHA's vision is to make effective communication accessible and achievable for all. Effective communication encompasses skills in speech, language, cognition, and social communication.

Speech-language pathologists identify, assess, diagnose, and treat communication disorders in children and adults. Children with autism have social communication deficits and often have other speech and language challenges; speech-language pathologists can address these needs. Because

BCBA professionals also are involved with children with autism, there can be frequent interface between speech-language pathologists and ABA therapists.

ASHA's vice president for Government Relations and Public Policy, Joan Mele-McCarthy, DA, CCC-SLP indicated that, "ASHA members have major concerns that ABA practitioners are writing IEP goals for speech, language, and social communication and providing speech and language services without the involvement of speech-language pathologists. ASHA-certified speech-language pathologists have the qualifications to provide such services for individuals with communication disorders. They have a master's or doctoral degree, pass a national exam, and participate in mandatory continuing education activities. They have the education and experience to understand the theoretical basis and neurobiological substrates for communication" (Joan Mele-McCarthy, personal communication, August 6, 2015).

Judith Page, PhD, CCC-SLP, ASHA's Immediate Past President, stressed that "speech-language pathologists need to be involved whenever individuals have communication disorders. This is a major concern for ASHA members" (Judith Page, personal communication, August 6, 2015).

For a number of years, ASHA has heard from speech-language pathologists that they are being excluded from service provision, are not being included on IEP teams, and that ABA therapists are often the only service providers for children with autism spectrum disorder. ASHA is concerned that many children with autism are not receiving the speech, language, and social communication services they need from highly qualified and appropriately credentialed professionals.

Diane Paul, PhD, CCC-SLP, ASHA's Director of Clinical Issues in Speech-Language Pathology, indicated that "ASHA has concerns when the mandates of IDEA and other laws are not applied; when access to services is denied; when there is exclusive use of any intervention, such as ABA; and when speech-language pathologists are not included in services for individuals who have communication problems. IDEA requires that services be individualized. Making a priori decisions to use ABA for all children is inconsistent with IDEA's mandate of an individualized and free, appropriate, public education" (Diane Paul, personal communication, August 6, 2015).

ASHA wanted the Department of Education to be aware of these concerns and wanted the Department to inform educators. Early in 2015, ASHA arranged a meeting with Department of Education personnel and alerted them to the concerns of speech-language pathologists. On July 6, 2015, Melody Musgrove, Director of the Office of Special Education Programs in the U.S. Department of Education's Office of Special Education and Rehabilitative Services, issued a "Dear Colleague" letter. In part, the letter reads:

> It has come to our attention that there are concerns in the field regarding services delivered to children with autism spectrum disorder (ASD). In particular, the Office of Special Education Programs (OSEP) has received reports that a growing number of children with ASD may not be receiving needed speech and language services, and that speech-language pathologists and other appropriate professionals may not be included in evaluation and eligibility determinations. . . . Some IDEA programs may be including applied behavior analysis (ABA) therapists exclusively without including, or considering input from, speech-language pathologists and other professionals who provide different types of specific therapies that may be appropriate for children with ASD when identifying IDEA services for children with ASD. . . .
>
> We recognize that ABA therapy is just one methodology used to address the needs of children with ASD and remind States and local programs to ensure that decisions regarding services are made based on the unique needs of each individual child with a disability (and the child's family in the case of Part C of the IDEA). (U.S. Department of Education 2015)

And it is not just the exclusion of speech-language pathologists in the IEP process that has ASHA concerned about the exclusive use of ABA. Mele-McCarthy noted, "ABA is a single way to intervene with a population of individuals who project certain types of behavior. It is one approach. Speech-language pathology services are based on an eclectic body of scientific knowledge that allows one to understand the basic neurobiological foundations for communication, the developmental trajectory, the specific components of communication disorders, and the array of scientifically based treatments that can be applied to intervention.

"ABA is a single methodology," Mele-McCarthy continued. "The full spectrum of speech-language pathology services is informed by a body of knowledge based upon integrated, organic systems that have a typical development trajectory from which different kinds of interventions, strategies, and methodologies have been developed and ratified through science. We are concerned for the people that we serve because a single approach is very limiting" (Joan Mele-McCarthy, personal communication, August 6, 2015).

Judith Page summed up ASHA's concern and message with regard to ABA. "A core characteristic of autism is difficulty with social communication, which is within the domain of speech-language pathologists. It is critical that speech-language pathologists be involved with this population so that individuals with autism receive the full spectrum of services they need" (Judith Page, personal communication, August 6, 2015).

Just as ASHA objects to applied behavior analysis and its practitioners as the only available intervention, the wake created by the advance of ABA has pushed many scholars and practitioners in related fields into the quiet backwaters of science. One such person is Gerard Costa of Montclair State University. "I think the problem with ABA and the problem with what's happened in terms of autism, viewed as an 'illness' and termed an 'epidemic' and seen as a social ill, is that behavior analysts have convinced people that autism is a behavioral disorder that needs to be treated with behavioral approaches.

"Autism is not a disorder of behavior. It is a difference in the structure, functioning, and processing of the human brain that affects everything from memory to communication to self-regulation, so social relationships and our approach to autism must therefore be guided by a much broader array of sciences including the sciences of neurology, physiology, occupational therapy, physical therapy, and speech-language pathology."

Costa continued, "One of the frameworks I have embraced and have been part of for about 16 years has been a model developed by the late Dr. Stanley Greenspan. He was one of my teachers and mentors, and I currently serve as a member of the Board of Directors for the organization he founded called Interdisciplinary Council on Development and Learning (ICDL). He developed a model with a colleague of his, Dr. Serena Wieder, known as the DIRFloortime Model, which stands for developmental, individual-differences, and relationship-based approaches.

"We have a graduate certificate program here at Montclair State University on developmental models of autism intervention that emphasizes multidisciplinary thinking. It has been a core part of my life for the past 15 to 20 years," noted Costa. "I think this is much more than ABA has ever adequately addressed. I think the whole claim for evidence that is made by ABA is absolutely an erroneous assertion in a true sense of what science is about. Essentially it's this: What you define as measurable is determined by your theory, and if your theory only looks at the behavior, behavior is all you will measure and think about.

"I continue to teach and talk about Thomas Kuhn and his book, *The Structure of Scientific Revolutions*, which proposes that science is not only about science, but that sometimes it is also primarily about economics and politics. God forgive me, but I believe so strongly that autism and the field of autism are controlled by economic, political, and ideological forces rather than by science.

"I'm generally a real optimist, but I am cynical about ABA's claim that all they do is based in science," explained Costa. "I have been at meetings where strident ideologues have said, 'I tell parents everything I do is based in science.' That's the arrogance, the hubris that has emerged in the field of ABA, because they claim that they are filled with science and yet ignore the long history of alternate perspectives and evidence in developmental science; in language development; in occupational therapy; in education, especially on inclusion; and in the neurosciences.

"They have carved out their view of autism as being all about changing behavior—that there is nothing inside that we have to address or that there are other ways of looking at the human. Many ABA therapists argue that we don't need occupational therapists, we don't need physical therapists, and we don't need speech-language pathologists. This perspective deprives students of access to the general education curriculum and instead uses ABA curricula in which students must master each skill before moving on to the next without concern as to why they may not be able to master a skill."

Costa continued, "I have been in early intervention since 1985. I've heard people ask, 'Why wouldn't I do the best thing for my child? Why wouldn't I do what science tells me?' So the oppressive discourse has made it impossible for some families to separate education and science from propaganda. I think Autism Speaks and other organizations have failed to be open to the wider array of science. I hope this is changing. They have co-opted a particular discourse and created both a literature and a marketing campaign that convinces families this is the only way. In doing so, they have ensured the industry of behavior therapists a supply of customers.

"Whether or not it is helping children is becoming secondary, especially when there is a growing body of contrary evidence. In 2013, Dr. Thomas Insel, the then executive director of the National Institute for Mental Health (NIMH), stated clearly that the field cannot solely look at symptoms when there is a large body of information about the neurology of autism. I know this is provocative, but I think some advocacy organizations are looking at autism in a way that's well-suited for the economic, political, and ideological engines that have developed around the field. Nonetheless, I don't dispute that these organizations and approaches were developed to help children and families, but they have not relinquished approaches that no longer address the underlying problem. The history of science and medicine has been about changing treatments as we learn more.

"The unfortunate truth has been defined in the larger field by codifying procedures, insurance reimbursements, treatments, protocols, and literature from mainstream ABA that has codified a way of looking at autism," noted Costa. "I think this has been so incredibly damaging for many children. Yet I know, understand, and respect the fact that many parents will say, 'ABA gave my child a little bit.' I need to be able to connect with those parents. My view is that ABA is not wrong but that its uses have been wrong. ABA is not a disciplinary field of study. It is a method. It is a learning approach. It is *not* a discipline. We all learn from reinforcements. We all learn from structured ways. But autism is not a behavioral disorder. It is a different structure, functioning, and processing of the human brain."

Costa continued, "I believe it was Ivar Lovaas's (the major proponent of ABA) authentic wish to contribute greatly. In so many ways his is a noble contribution to the field. His behavioral approaches gave families a sense of hope and contributed to the idea that children can be helped and that families can engage with their children. Lovaas was an enormously wonderful, engaging, warm, and affect-rich person, and his contribution led the field away from the uses of aversives such as water-misting and electric shock, a method he had earlier employed.

"The problem was that science changed, but the behaviorists didn't. We began learning so much more in the late '80s, '90s, and the 2000s—the 'decade of the brain'—about what was going on in the brain. We were developing much more insights from other disciplines. Lucy Miller, Stanley Greenspan, Daniel Stern, Stuart Shanker, and many others began to change the field of developmental theory and developmental understanding, and they have changed the field of autism. The problem was the behaviorists thought that they were the only ones in heaven.

"It used to be that there were five subtypes of autism," noted Costa. "Now there is autism spectrum disorder. It's a failure in diagnostics. Autism has come to mean too many different things. It covers behaviors and symptoms that likely originate from such a diverse set of circumstances and underlying differences that I think it has lost meaning. I don't think autism makes any sense as a term. It adds value in a codified world, where if you have that label you can get more services or an insurance company will reimburse you, but that's the tail wagging the dog.

"In *The Structure of Scientific Revolutions*, Kuhn writes about dominant paradigms exercising their power and becoming *the* paradigm through which world views are explained. At some point, however, events are being recorded that the dominant paradigm doesn't adequately explain. Behavioral approaches do not adequately explain things. Even behaviorists have to acknowledge there is a lot more stuff going on than they can explain.

"I don't think the behavioral approach can remain a dominant paradigm as we learn more about autism and human development. I don't think they're here to stay. In the near future, we will see the field of autism not dominated by ABA or behavioral approaches, but it's not going to be a pleasant break-up."

Costa noted, "As far as I am aware, no state has mandated or required or even encouraged the DIR certificate issued by ICDL for people hired within educational systems or health systems. The preeminence of the BACB has made it difficult for other perspectives to step in and has diminished the ability for educators to teach by integrating attunement and self-regulation as intrinsic elements of the teaching relationship, not to be surrendered to behavioral specialists. This culture of the scientific community in autism has been a very exclusive one and has been a detriment to broadening services for families and for people with autism.

"At the same time that behavioral approaches have become the dominant approach in autism, a host of federal initiatives have emphasized much broader ways of thinking about the child that are much more about understanding the forces that influence development and learning. This includes a shift in how we think about 'disabilities,' and particularly autism, toward a strengths-based perspective embracing inclusion and neurodiversity.

"The Every Student Succeeds Act, the successor of No Child Left Behind, embraces a broader understanding of 'evidenced-based' so that educators are prepared to work with more neurodiverse groups of children using strategies like universal design for learning (UDL) and positive behavior supports (PBS). These approaches are rooted in understanding the nature of learning, developmental, and behavioral difficulties and in enhancing the child's ability to communicate their needs—not simply stopping socially determined behaviors," explained Costa. "Transdisciplinary teamwork by the professionals already in our schools—OTs, PTs, SLPs, mental health specialists, and teachers—must be provided with the right type of professional formation and mentorship.

"We have to be honest enough with ourselves in recognizing that the 'act' of science is not simply an academic or high-level, moral inquiry. We would be foolish to ignore the economic motivations. The BACB, once developed as a way of ensuring quality and effectiveness, has become a guild protecting an industry" (Gerard Costa, personal communication, March 11, 2016).

AND FROM HERE SCHOOLS MOVE FORWARD

While to some it might seem that behavior analysts are taking over, for others building the profession of behavior analysis is more like Sisyphus continually pushing a stone uphill. "Our field is still young, but it is growing rapidly," noted Gina Green, executive director of APBA. "But the education system has its own set of laws. It's not just behavior analysis; state recognition of a profession in the form of a licensure law often has no effect on the education system unless the education laws or rules are changed so that they recognize that license.

"When a state approves licensure for behavior analysts, there is typically no requirement for the education system in that state to recognize that license, to my knowledge. That is, the behavior analyst license is not automatically a qualification for holding a position within the public schools," Green explained. "So we have to go back to the legislature or to the education system and say, 'Please add this state license to the list of credentials that you will accept for positions within the public schools.' There are only five states that have anything remotely like that so far. Twenty-five states have passed laws to license behavior analysts, and that needs to be the first objective in many states. It is difficult enough to get a law passed to license behavior analysts. Going to the education system in those states and saying, 'Okay, now that we have this license, please add it to your list of recognized credentials,' is down the road in most states" (Gina Green, personal communication, July 14, 2015).

Waiting for formal acknowledgment of licensure for BCBAs is not holding some states back from moving forward. Utah State University Professor Thomas Higbee said, "We are in a period of rapid growth for BCBAs in Utah, and it is driven almost exclusively by changes in Medicaid policy and now insurance funding. Most of that growth has happened in the last five years since the Medicaid waiver was put in place. I'm not aware of any behavior analyst who is looking for a job that doesn't have one right now."

Higbee continued, "Many BCBAs in other states are working outside of the educational system. In Utah many school districts are hiring BCBAs or encouraging their existing behavioral specialists and autism specialists to go into BCBA programs and continue working in the districts. Within Utah, most of the larger districts will have one to five BCBAs on staff working as coordinators for their self-contained severe units or autism teams, autism specialists, or behavior specialists.

"BCBAs are fantastically productive and are an excellent resource for the districts. Bringing all that a behavior analyst has to offer to public schools, there's incredible value in that. When I worked in California, all the BCBAs were working pretty much as either independent contractors or working for agencies that contracted with public schools to offer services."

Higbee is also confident about the research base of behavior analysis. "I point to hundreds of published empirical articles behind, not only the individual therapeutic interventions, but also package combination interventions. Behavior analysis is a basic science. We're continually evolving.

"I've been in this field for almost 20 years, and what I'm doing now is very different than what I did at the beginning, because the analysis part of behavior analysis is that we are constantly and critically self-evaluating what we're doing in the development of new and better therapeutic techniques. In my clinical programs, we are collecting and analyzing hundreds of data points every day for every single kid in the program to evaluate their progress. There is a strong scientific foundation in everything we do, and a good behavior analyst can point that out for every technique they are using" (Thomas Higbee, personal communication, August 11, 2015).

Similar to the experience in Utah, special educators in other states are being encouraged to return to school for behavior analysis. Margaret Masimore is a former director of special education for the Metropolitan Nashville Public Schools and remembered a similar rite of passage some 20 years ago. "Back in the early '90s when I first became special education director, Metro contracted with agencies for occupational and physical therapy at the tune of multiple millions of dollars every year."

Masimore explained, "We contracted because those professionals held a medical license and not teacher certification. Therefore, according to the mentality of the pencil pushers and the budget people, Metro couldn't pay a competitive rate. Those professionals would have to get paid like an educational assistant or a paraprofessional, instead of the higher salary they could command as a contractor. So, we couldn't hire anybody.

"Then we did a lot of data collecting, looking at competitive salaries and how much money we would save if we hired experts, and we were able to get the salaries up and had our own in-house people as occupational and physical therapists. And now we are doing the same thing with behavior analysts. As a result, there are more and more special education teachers going back and getting ABA certification" (Margaret Masimore, personal communication, June 17, 2015).

Many BCBAs are entering the workforce through either the health care or education door. This dualism creates opportunities for employment but presents a complicated landscape for the profession to navigate. APBA's Green related, "The education system has its own rules. This is all part of the politics and the legalities of autism service delivery, and it is part of what makes things very fragmented. Health insurance legislation brings in another huge set of political issues. Like education, the health insurance industry and insurance laws are different state to state.

"Several of the autism insurance laws specify that the availability of health insurance coverage for services for kids with autism in no way relieves the education system of its responsibilities, but school districts' responsibilities are limited to educational objectives. Typically health insurance does not have to—and will not—pay for services that are deemed educational," noted Green. "It is a major part of the battle to get health insurance to pay for ABA, because some insurance companies contend that ABA is educational and that they do not pay for educational services—that is the school's responsibility. Then, of course, many schools don't fully embrace and deliver ABA services either. That leaves kids in limbo.

"We have had to develop arguments, counterarguments, and supporting research to refute this claim by the health insurance industry that ABA is strictly educational. We now need to cast it as medically necessary treatment, and that means using entirely different language, a different way of talking about ABA as medical treatment. You can't use education words when you're advocating for health insurance coverage" (Gina Green, personal communication, July 14, 2015).

REFERENCE

U.S. Department of Education, Office of Special Education and Rehabilitative Services. 2015, July 6. "Dear Colleague" Letter. Retrieved from http://www2.ed.gov/policy/speced/guid/idea/memosdcltrs/dclspeechlanguageautism0706153q2015.pdf.

Chapter Seven

Pervasive Inertia

If we're talking about children who need accelerated growth and children with significant mental health needs, that is not an individual school's responsibility.

—Patricia Fagan Greco

My vision is that every special education department will have BCBAs as part of their leadership and clinical teams to improve services for all kids with behavioral and academic challenges.

—Thomas Higbee

Menomonee Falls, Wisconsin, Superintendent Patricia Fagan Greco has lived the prescient statement of President Ford. "Thirty years ago, I used to sit in IEP meetings where people would say out loud, 'Your child is never going to college.' Or they would say, 'These are skills that he will never be able to achieve.' We know so much more now about how kids learn. Today we know that there are children in special education with a full range of abilities.

"We have to figure out the strategies that are going to hook them deeper into the learning environment. Yet, it is hard to find special educators, let alone people who have specific skills sets. We'll get 800 to 1,000 applicants for an elementary position, whereas we might get 20 for an opening in special education. We don't have the appropriate supply and demand for special education in general."

Fagan Greco continued, "Today we are reducing staff rather than hiring staff. And the level of expectation has doubled in the last five years. When you look at expectations for student performance and how schools are measured, no one is taking into account the range and need of the student body. We're losing sight of the needs of the children: How do we actually work together across agencies? How do we actually have a deeper conversation around how schools can bridge to success after school for all the children we serve?

"School systems are complex learning organizations and very few people are connecting them to the work around how hospitals have demonstrated the ability to replicate and scale improvement that goes across countries," noted Fagan Greco. "We talk about improvement as if it belongs to an individual school. We are having the wrong conversation. If we're talking about children who need accelerated growth and children with significant mental health needs, that is not an individual school's responsibility.

"We have to think much deeper as a country around what our core values are. Schools embrace every learner, yet we have organizations across communities that serve different functions with resource bases behind them all targeted on how to make that community healthy. Our special needs children and their families are a part of that. But we are not connecting the dots" (Patricia Fagan Greco, personal communication, July 23, 2015).

THEORY VERSUS PRACTICE

Nina Gupta, an Atlanta-based school district attorney, understands Superintendent Fagan Greco's worries about the lack of collaboration among schools and agencies focused on children and adults with special needs. And Gupta also sees courts addressing the needs of children with autism in a way that is different and more activist in approach than their treatment of other disabilities.

"I see unique to autism cases, courts and judges willing to really get into the weeds of what best practices are and not really leaving that to sound educational discretion," explained Gupta. "They're bringing in best practices from BCBAs and from pediatricians and developmental pediatricians. As opposed to your EBD kids and your OHI kids and all of your other exceptionalities, where the courts focus on what do the educators have to say, when you're talking about kids with autism, the courts are going outside that scope to inform what should be happening in a schoolhouse. I see a trend, a blurring of the educational model and a medical model for kids with autism. It means a whole lot of money is going to be expended by school districts."

Gupta continued, "Autism is the tip of the spear because it's not only an exceptionality, it's also a diagnosis. I have never seen anything like it. There's been such a rapid increase in the diagnosis of autism. The autism advocacy community has been so effective in coalescing, gathering support, and getting the issue in front of people. Everyone has been touched by autism in one way or another.

"Those two things put together—(1) that it's a diagnosis, and (2) the dramatic increase of it—make autism uniquely situated to have its own jurisprudence, for lack of a better word, under IDEA. As the science of disability and as our knowledge of disability progresses, the case law is not necessarily going to keep up. Legislation is too slow of an animal. Government can't keep up, but case law can or at least is better positioned to keep up. Using the example of EBD, as we learn more about the science of mental illness and treatment for mental illness, I can certainly see the case law moving in that direction as well. I don't think we're there yet with any other exceptionality, but I can see that kind of thing developing in the future" (Nina Gupta, personal communication, June 22, 2015).

APBA's Gina Green became a behavior analyst in the 1980s and has no problem with the special education hearing process getting into the weeds and pulling in practices from ABA. The disregard for established science around applied behavior analysis and other approaches to autism has been a great frustration for her for many years. "It's maddening. It's been an obstacle to progress for a long, long time. It's one of the reasons that a group of parents and professionals, of which I was a part, founded the Association for Science in Autism Treatment (ASAT) in the mid-1990s. We saw that, at that time, there was no organization disseminating scientifically accurate information about autism diagnosis or autism treatment. So much time and energy and money was being wasted on interventions that didn't have any basis in science or logic and on some that had proven ineffective and even harmful."

Green continued, "So we started the Association for Science and Autism Treatment to provide that kind of information. ASAT has advisors from several disciplines, and its mission all of these years has been to disseminate scientifically sound information about autism and autism treatments. On the ASAT website (www.asatonline.org) you can find good, succinct summaries of the scientific research on all kinds of treatments. There is also some good information to help parents and others evaluate claims about treatments that they may encounter on the internet or at conferences, parent support groups, and so on.

"My interactions with the public education system have mainly been as an expert for parents who disagreed with their school districts regarding appropriate services for their children with autism. I was often in the role of helping parents advocate for their children to get ABA services, either in a private school or via home-based services if they were little kids," explained Green. "I ran into the occasional special education director who was very supportive and understood that the district didn't have the resources and the expertise to provide truly effective services. But that has been fairly rare, in my experience. More often the public school's stance was, 'We have a fine program for your child. You should not question us or doubt that our program is appropriate and effective'" (Gina Green, personal communication, July 14, 2015).

The state of Florida recognized the value of ABA and passed a law that allows Board Certified Behavior Analysts hired by parents access into public schools. The 2015–2016 school year marked the third year of guaranteed admittance for these privately engaged BCBAs who may attend IEP meetings, observe a student in the classroom, and collaborate with district personnel.

Matt Briere-Saltis is one such BCBA. He works in the northeast corner of the state, particularly in the Duval County Public Schools (Jacksonville). "I get to see a lot of different variations in the schools' interpretation of what ABA is, what autism is, what supports ABA can and should provide, and how the collaboration with the school should happen. On the positive side, I see a lot of openness to the idea of collaboration and support from the ABA providers in the community who are working with kids on the spectrum in the public and private school systems.

"One of the most meaningful opportunities that BCBAs are just now getting is the chance to provide a consistent voice within the classroom setting, where I know the school districts are working very hard to identify, hire, and train the appropriate personnel in ABA modalities," noted Briere-Saltis. "But it's difficult because a lot of the teachers and the paraprofessionals that are working directly with our kids for 40 hours a week are not necessarily trained in ABA or provided a lot of support or supporting-documentation information on how ABA can specifically be applied in a classroom setting for kids with autism.

"I find teachers are typically given some cursory information. They might get training during the summer or in the school year where they get introduced to certain ideas, certain topics, certain strategies—interventions that are wonderful in theory but are very different and difficult in application. What I'm finding is that the BCBAs who get an opportunity to work with those professionals in the school setting and are able to be there on a consistent basis, even if it's once a week, sometimes two or three times a week, can provide specific feedback or modeling on just how specific interventions or strategies really are applied to students with autism."

Briere-Saltis continued, "Once a BCBA achieves vendor status, you are given a badge that you present whenever you go to the schools. You log in on a computer system so the school has data regarding when you are there, when you sign in and sign out, and you have to get some confirmation from the school, whether it's the principal, the vice principal, the classroom teacher, or the autism site coach at that particular school. Each school has its own way of doing it, but the policy really dictates that the administration has to collaborate with the provider on appropriate times and places.

"My experience has been that once the family establishes that they want this support to exist and the provider has gone through and received vendor status, the schools really do a very good job of working with the clinician to identify what the appropriate dates and times are to provide support," noted Briere-Saltis. "The problem the BCBA is there to address is causing the teachers, and typically some of the classmates, distress because there's a child with needs that are not being met. The payer source for the service is either the family's private insurance or an out-of-pocket expense for the family, so the schools work with the BCBA.

"Teachers are typically very receptive of the support. The administration, once they have all their ducks in a row, is comfortable allowing the clinicians to come in and provide that support. This is the third year that the law has existed in Florida. Early on we saw a lot of trepidation, a lot of basic misunderstanding of what behavior analysis is and what role the clinician was going to play in the classroom setting. Now that it's been a couple of years, I think a lot of those misconceptions have been ironed out."

Briere-Saltis continued, "With Florida being one of the original birthplaces of ABA, we are a little bit spoiled in that almost everyone has heard of it. Even if they don't have a great understanding, they are at least aware of behavior analysis. I certainly do run into, especially in the rural areas, a lack of understanding, a lack of awareness, which I am certain is related to limited access to services, but I would say these instances are becoming fewer and further between.

"During the process of getting the legislation pushed through, we fought hard to make certain that BCBAs would be allowed to provide feedback to the teachers, specifically during outside-of-school hours, so feedback would not happen in the middle of the classroom. You don't want to stop the class to give the teacher feedback. In our feedback, we cannot necessarily dictate what the teachers do or don't do, but we are given the opportunity and afforded the time to provide feedback to the teachers and to the administrators as well," explained Briere-Saltis. "The most effective application of this legislation and of ABA within a public school setting that I've seen is when you have an administrator, a teacher, a BCBA, and a parent all on the same page, all working within the confines of the IEP" (Matt Briere-Saltis, personal communication, September 15, 2015).

Keith Hersh is a BCBA who has worked with school districts, in a role similar to Matt Briere-Saltis, in Broward and Brevard counties in Florida, Jefferson County (Louisville) in Kentucky, and in rural counties in Kentucky and southern Indiana. "I have interfaced with various school systems in multiple states and have seen a great deal of variance as a BCBA and professional consultant regarding the types of involvement I have in public school settings when trying to serve children on the spectrum. I believe that the administration either has an open or closed door policy before I step into the school or begin involvement."

Hersh continued, "Commonly I've been told things like, 'It's a HIPAA violation for the other students,' which is a valid concern that certainly should be addressed but also should not be used as an excuse to end the involvement process. From my experience, schools that issue those types of statements up front are typically what I consider closed off, not open to collaboration with external consultants. I've also been told by multiple school districts that no one can evaluate a teacher except for administrative officials within the school.

"That obviously leads to challenges because I typically observe—measure in some way, shape, or form—how people are reacting to a student's behavior," explained Hersh. "If I cannot determine how they are reacting and what socially mediated consequences they apply for various behavioral challenges and behavioral deficits, it becomes extremely difficult to do my job, which is to help create an environment that has very prescribed consequences for particular behaviors that we either want to increase or decrease."

Hersh offered an example of where he interfaced with a school on behalf of a family of an elementary school child in a mainstream classroom who was manifesting challenging behaviors at school including noncompliance with instructions, physical aggression toward teachers and peers, and screaming episodes. The child was being suspended from school frequently. "The family felt that the child had made significant progress at home with behavioral interventions and wondered if the same interventions were being utilized at school. My job was to work with the school and see what types of consequences were being delivered as the challenging behaviors actually happened in the classroom or on the playground."

Even though Hersh, the school staff, and the family worked together and reduced the problem behaviors of the student in this particular case and in many others, he still meets with resistance from many schools. "If I were an employee of the school, there would be a different level of acceptance to my feedback and involvement, an increase in the amount of acceptance. At this point in time, behavior analysts must first earn the confidence and the trust of the schools and demonstrate that they are there to help; they must show that they are not a threat" (Keith Hersh, personal communication, June 29, 2015).

Moving toward easy access to and ready acceptance of behavior analysts on the part of public schools across the country is something that Thomas Higbee, BCBA-D and professor at Utah State University, would like to see. "I have worked very hard within the system in the state of Utah to improve special education and improve the capacity of special educators and special education systems to provide effective services for kids on the autism spectrum.

"We have clear empirical evidence showing that gains, and in some cases quite dramatic gains, can be produced with intensive behavioral intervention; knowing that there is a window of opportunity for many children, there is a great need for rapid and aggressive advocacy. We've produced some great results with districts, and I would hold up our district programs against any private program in terms of the quality and fidelity of implementation. There are evidence-based approaches and programs available within public school systems.

Higbee continued, "We have gone from fewer than 20 BCBAs, which mostly included me and my colleagues at the university and our graduate students, to about 150 BCBAs in Utah. My vision is that every special education department will have BCBAs as part of their leadership and clinical teams to improve services for all kids with behavioral and academic challenges. My professional experience has been in California and Utah, and the cultures of those two states are very different. It is very rare that families will go through due process in Utah. There's a culture of collaboration between parents and school districts" (Thomas Higbee, personal communication, August 11, 2015).

PARENTS: IDEA'S COMPLIANCE POLICE

While, in Higbee's view, special education due process is a rarity in Utah, it is not a rarity in many other states. Miriam Kurtzig Freedman is an attorney in Boston and represents public school districts on special education matters. She was a hearing officer for eight years and a public school teacher early in her career and feels that among IDEA's structural shortcomings is that it relies on parents to enforce the law. "It forces parents to 'advocate' for their child *against* their schools" (Freedman 2012, 16). Freedman wrote, "IDEA, premised on corrosive distrust rather than pedagogy, created a complicated system of federal, state, and local requirements, and has spawned a host of unintended consequences, full of dilemmas for educators, parents, and citizens" (Freedman 2012, 8). Freedman also takes issue with IDEA as a "twentieth-century input- rights-driven law, not a twenty-first century output- or results-driven law" (Freedman 2012, 8).

There are tens of thousands of parents who understand that IDEA relies on parental enforcement and that it pits the parents against the school district, but few have lived it to the extent of Sherry Smith. Smith was enrolled at the University of Michigan, studying political science and planning to attend law school, when her son was diagnosed with cognitive impairment. At that point, Smith and her husband made a major decision: he would work to support the family and she would focus on caring for their son and learning all she could about special education and cognitive impairment. She left the University of Michigan a year short of earning a bachelor's degree.

"I spent my days researching sections of IDEA," noted Smith. "I spent hours finding and printing pieces of this overwhelming law that I believed were potentially applicable to my son. Then at night, when everyone was sound asleep, I would sit in bed with pencils, highlighters, and a clipboard reviewing and selecting relevant parts of IDEA. Then, because the law is so complicated and because words matter and are up for interpretation, especially in IDEA, I decided that it was time to start attending workshops and seminars to help me unravel IDEA. I would travel a couple of hours and spend the night away from home just to attend an all-day crash-course seminar about special education law."

Smith continued, "I would go to Wrightslaw seminars, I would go to the west side of Michigan, I would go to Ohio—anything during the course of 14 years that I thought could give me even a nugget of understanding in order to boost my confidence and comfort level while sitting in an IEP meeting. Before that, I felt so overwhelmed. The teachers and administrators would use terminology and acronyms that I did not know. I had no clue what they meant; no idea. I felt so out of place, out of my comfort zone, out of my element, and I don't like feeling that way as a mom. You are supposed to grab the reins in raising your children, and I felt like I had no control. I was overwhelmed.

"But I slowly started to gain confidence and gain knowledge and gain understanding; that was a turning point in my family's life, in my son's education," explained Smith. "I was finally able to go in and truly participate as a team member; I was better equipped. I was able to maneuver important services into his IEP, and the IEP team suddenly started to take me seriously. They didn't run the show. We worked more collaboratively as a team, and this worked out pretty well, at least on paper. I walked away from those IEP meetings feeling great. My son was now getting occupational therapy, he was getting speech, and he was assigned a paraprofessional to assist in modifying curriculum. All of these services looked great on paper.

"But then I learned that you also have to be a watchdog and make sure that these services are actually happening in the school. It was one thing to have something on paper, to make a parent happy, and send them away saying, 'Okay, don't you worry now,' patting me on the head, but it came to my attention that they were not delivering what they had promised. So, I filed a formal complaint with the Michigan Department of Education because the school district was not following my son's IEP."

Smith continued, "After the complaint and the state agreeing with me, the school district hired new staff and they got their act together. But during the last couple of years, I felt that I was no longer a part of the team. I knew that the district was making decisions outside of the IEP meeting. It was pretty obvious. When you go into a meeting to discuss changing of placement, which is a big deal, and it's not discussed as a team, and my input wasn't even acknowledged or considered, I knew that something had to have taken place outside of the IEP meeting.

"I wanted to be a part of those conversations. I could not figure out how they had reached their determination," Smith noted. "They told us where my son was going at the last placement meeting. I know that I'm supposed to be part of that decision-making process, and I was not. The school district would not explain how they had reached that determination, so I asked for the emails. I thought they had to have had communication among themselves. I thought let me be part of that—let me see how you reached that decision" (Sherry Smith, personal communication, August 5, 2015).

Smith requested 14 months of emails, starting with April 2014, from the district under the Freedom of Information Act and received a letter three weeks later from the superintendent in response. The superintendent's letter stated that the school district "believes the total cost to fulfill this FOIA will be $77,718.75" and asked that Smith "please forward a deposit of no less than 50 percent of the estimated total" if she wanted the school to proceed with the request (Goodrich Area Schools, personal communication, June 10, 2015). "For the first time," Smith noted, "I had to enlist the help of an attorney, and suddenly I received hundreds of pages of transcripts and e-mails.

"I have been at this for 15 years. We have a weak advocacy network in my part of Michigan. We are middle-class Joes; I cut my dreams of a career short, and my job ended up being to learn about special education. Yet, after all these years, I say to my husband how much I feel for parents who can't do what we did. My heart goes out to them because I know there are parents who wish they could do more but they just can't" (Sherry Smith, personal communication, August 5, 2015). The superintendent and school board president of the Goodrich Area Schools did not respond to repeated offers to participate in the research for this book.

Judith Ursitti, the Texan who found a far more hospitable environment for her son in Massachusetts, empathizes with families facing the decision of whether or not to engage attorneys to fight the school district. "When my son was turning 3, my husband and I had to decide if we were going to allow him to be placed in a substandard public school program and hire an attorney to pursue litigation or if we were going to spend that money on therapy.

"We had to decide if we were willing to risk his future and spend the money on legal fees because he was at that window of opportunity where early interventions are meaningful. When parents have to make that decision it empowers the school systems because parents are in a corner. Most families cannot afford to pay out-of-pocket for meaningful interventions and sue at the same time."

Ursitti continued, "Children like my son are not being sent to early intervention, they are being sent to the public school program and very, very few public schools are equipped to handle this type of disability. The worst thing about it is that the child is not accessing the appropriate care and his or her future is being limited. The taxpayer is also getting a greater burden because the child is not reaching full potential and will need more lifetime support and services. It's a penny wise and pound foolish practice by states, municipalities, and school districts" (Judith Ursitti, personal communication, August 6, 2015).

REFERENCE

Freedman, M. K. 2012. "Special Education: Its Ethical Dilemmas, Entitlement Status, and Suggested Systemic Reforms." *The University of Chicago Law Review* 79(1): 1–24: Online Exclusive. Retrieved from https://lawreview.uchicago.edu/sites/lawreview.uchicago.edu/files/uploads/79_1/Freedman.pdf.

Chapter Eight

Disconnected Services, Disconnected Funding

If we think about the end game, it influences what we do now in early intervention.

—Stephan Viehweg

I would like to see the integration of an ABA framework within the context of a public school.

—Erin Maguire

"I have spent the last 10 years trying to get insurance to the table in all 50 states," reflected Lorri Unumb of Autism Speaks. "Now that we're almost there, the next step in the journey is to figure out how to blend together all those sources of support. Schools can't slough off their responsibilities just because we now have health insurance; that is not acceptable. It wasn't acceptable for health insurance to not be at the table or to push off their obligations, and it isn't acceptable for schools to now step away from the table. There needs to be a concerted effort to figure out the best way to get all the parties playing in the sandbox together nicely and just what the division of responsibility should be" (Lorri Unumb, personal communication, July 18, 2016).

Coordinating services, responsibilities, and funding for children with autism is a significant need. Many parents are unaware that there is a mandate for schools to provide services for preschool children with handicapping conditions. According to the Centers for Disease Control and Prevention (2015), "ASD can sometimes be detected at 18 months or younger. By age 2, a diagnosis by an experienced professional can be considered very reliable. However, many children do not receive a final diagnosis until much older. This delay means that children with an ASD might not get the help they need."

Not getting the help needed as early as possible has severe consequences for children with ASD, especially those on the more severe end of the scale. The "Child Find" component of Part C of IDEA is intended to ensure that very young children with developmental issues are found, diagnosed, and served by public school districts and other public agencies. If Part C actually worked, the level of autism advocacy may have been reduced. But Part C is spottily implemented and woefully under-enforced. That is why the autism community has pushed so strongly for parents and professionals to be aware of early warning signs and to move as quickly as possible. This is also why the autism community has pushed so strongly for insurance benefits to cover screenings, diagnosis, and treatments.

Unumb's desire to coordinate sources of support and responsibilities could not come fast enough for many parents. Public funding sources and services, special education, medical insurance, and private resources are disconnected. There are unnatural and arbitrary breakpoints in available services: between IDEA Part C to Part B, elementary school to high school, high school to rehabilitation services or employment. After high school children fall off an already rocky funding cliff and into the shaky world of adult services and supports.

Often something that is working well for a child has to stop when the child reaches an existing breakpoint in services. A new service picks up the pieces and stumbles on with a different level and variety of supports. Children with ASD and children with many other handicapping conditions require a smooth coordination of services and supports in order to maximize opportunities; fluid transition is essential. The bumps and jolts families experience are primarily the result of a lack of coordination between agencies and programs.

THE PART C PART B SHUFFLE

James Carr, CEO of the BACB, sees gaps in the implementation of services designed to catch autism and other developmental issues as early as possible. Speaking from his perspective as a researcher and former educator, rather than as an official of the BACB, Carr noted, "Autism insurance legislation was not designed to supplant or replace treatment services provided in the schools but rather to recognize that most children, certainly children with autism, have needs that transcend the school day. There are needs in the community, needs around physical health and safety, and health plans were not covering those services.

"If a child is diagnosed at age 2 and needs services, the school services generally do not kick in until age 3," noted Carr. "The degree and intensity of those services really depend on the state where you reside. The gaps in coverage and services were the impetus for autism legislation, but I do not think the legislation was designed to remove the source of treatment from schools to outside parties.

"Better coordination would be helpful. Unfortunately, we do a poor job in the U.S. of coordinating between state departments. Children with special needs rely on a solid integration of services, but we have a fractured service system. We have birth through 2, we have preschool, and then we have school-age children. Our adult services are handled through a totally different state department, and we have private services that are available outside of school hours. It is a very complicated landscape, and I think that there are advocates right now trying to make sure that we have as much evidence-based treatment in all of these different systems, but, long term, we are going to need much better intersystem coordination" (James Carr, personal communication, June 30, 2015).

The transition between Part C and Part B of IDEA noted by Carr is a familiar issue across the country. "There are real differences between Part B and Part C. Under the early intervention of Part C, the focus is on the overall development of the child. Then, when a child reaches 3 years of age, Part B takes over and the focus becomes educational benefit rather than overall development. Part B is about access to and progress in general education," noted Margaret Masimore, former director of special education in Nashville. "I have seen lots of problems with transitioning between Part C and B. Ideally, it should be seamless, but the differences in both the requirements and focus of those two parts of IDEA create a lot of challenges for the district and even more for the parents" (Margaret Masimore, personal communication, June 17, 2015).

As a special education leader in California, Maureen O'Leary Burness frequently saw how parents reacted to their children's moving from Part C to Part B. "Part C separates out who serves our infants. In California we have both schools and our regional centers that contract with the Department of

Developmental Services as the primary providers for children. What was most prevalent in those conversations from the parent perspective during hearings was the fact that families would get services like ABA through the regional centers in the home for their infant once he or she was diagnosed with autism, but then at 3, the child would become the responsibility of the school district. It was always a big shock to the school system when parents would say, 'I want what my child had as an infant through the Department of Developmental Services, and I want the school district to provide it because it is now the district's responsibility at age 3.' It was always a huge, huge fight."

O'Leary Burness continued, "I think what it showed is that we have to have partnerships. Schools are responsible for the school day and for the educational piece, but children go home and have evening and night issues. I think that's what drove the autism community to say, 'We need medical care to supplement what we get through the IEP process'" (Maureen O'Leary Burness, personal communication, August 5, 2015).

For some disabilities, a special education versus a medical model leads to different types of services. Joan Mele-McCarthy of ASHA noted, "Autism is a complex disorder. Some children, when diagnosed early and who receive intensive interventions, turn the corner. It depends on the complexity of their issues and the intensity and specificities of their interventions.

"The state of the science is not specific enough to say 'Here is the umbrella disorder. Here are the specific components of that disorder. You have this much from column A, this much from column B, and this much from column C. Therefore, these kinds of interventions with this kind of specificity and intensity are going to do the job.' Autism does not have clear scientific protocols like many cancers do, for example, whereby it can be specified, 'this is the kind of cancer, and this is what you do for it.' We are striving for that specificity, but we are not there yet."

Mele-McCarthy noted, "People pay for services from a variety of sources. Parents who receive services for their children in the public school system will also go to the private sector to augment services. Hopefully, services are coordinated between the private and public sectors. They get the services in the public sector through IDEA, then go to the private sector and have their insurance cover it. This partnering may apply for a variety of disorders under IDEA. It is not unique to autism" (Joan Mele-McCarthy, personal communication, August 6, 2015).

WE HAVE ALL BEEN HERE BEFORE

Intense fervor travels with special education. The original intent of the federal law was to provide access to all students regardless of handicapping condition, and specifically to the 1 million children to whom the schoolhouse gate was closed before Public Law 94-142 went into effect in 1977. What happened a few years after implementation surprised many and illustrates the unintended consequences of the law as well as the frustration of millions of parents with public schools' inability to educate all children.

Vanderbilt's Douglas Fuchs remembers that surprise. "When the number of kids with learning disabilities increased—and it increased precipitously and then steadily for two decades from roughly 1975 to '95—it provoked tremendous outcry at the local level all the way up to the federal level, and there were a lot of reasons for the outcry. One of the reasons was simply the sheer numbers of kids. It was considered by many on its face as invalid and unwanted. There was a very strong sense that this label was being used and overused in a very inappropriate way with disastrous financial results.

"So now we have this precipitous rise in the autism category," noted Fuchs. "Not nearly as large a proportion of kids with disabilities have the autism label as students years ago who received a diagnosis of learning disability, but there is a very precipitous rise of autism. And nobody is questioning the scientific validity, or I should say very few people are questioning the validity of those numbers. Very few are going around saying that this is prima facie evidence of the invalidity and intellectual bankruptcy of the autism category, which is what the claims were and continue to be around the category of learning disability. Even behavior disorders and speech and language impairments have faced those criticisms."

Fuchs continued, "In part the difference is that there has been this strong sense among some that learning disability is a fundamentally spurious category. It is a category that was constructed to compensate for general education's failure to instruct otherwise healthy, relatively normal kids. Autism is not seen that way. Autism is seen as something real and valid, though there are academics who find the entire spectrum to be problematic in a classic measurement sense. Nonetheless, there is something fundamentally different about how people think about autism in relation to how people think about high-incidence disabilities.

"It might be useful to think about autism and Down syndrome together, not that they share the same etiologies or behavioral symptoms, but because

Down syndrome also has a very strong advocacy base," explained Fuchs. "You now see children and youth with Down syndrome frequently in the media. That is not coincidental; it is a very deliberate effort to normalize the lives of those kids to whatever extent may be possible. This is another manifestation of the power of advocacy" (Douglas Fuchs, personal communication, July 16, 2015).

There are structural parallels to the response within special education to the rise in the number of students with learning disabilities in the 1980s and 1990s and the current increase in students diagnosed with autism. Those structural parallels include a sense on the part of school districts of being overwhelmed with the increasing numbers of those identified with the handicapping condition, battles and resentment regarding the amount of funding required to respond to the challenge, uncertainties surrounding the veracity of the diagnosis, and failures on the part of school districts to comply with IDEA.

The research of David S. Mandell and colleagues further illustrates the disconnections present in autism supports and services. His 2010 study focused on "how county-level resources are associated with the identification of children with autism spectrum disorders (ASD) in Medicaid." The study observed the patchwork nature of how Medicaid and special education complement one another to serve children with autism and questioned how aggressively some counties are in their pursuit of enrolling qualified children with ASD. "States have set various policies to serve children with ASD through their Medicaid programs. . . . It is unclear, however, whether autism services offered through state Medicaid programs are a complement to the resources devoted to autism services delivered through the education system or whether they act as a substitute in places with fewer education resources" (Mandell, Morales, Xie, Polsky, Stahmer, and Marcus 2010, 1242).

Another issue on the autism front is the availability of BCBAs in public education. There are less than 20,000 BCBAs in the United States and around 15,000 school districts. That means that there are roughly 1.25 BCBAs per district, but, like nearly all other precious commodities, BCBAs are not evenly distributed. California has 3,799 BCBAs and BCaBAs, Florida 2,483, Georgia 337, Arizona 53, Mississippi 50, South Dakota 24, and Wyoming seven (Behavior Analyst Certification Board 2016). A combination of the availability of BCBAs and the cultural attitude toward special education make for wide variation in states' use of BCBAs in public education.

James Carr of the BACB noted, "A number of states, Louisiana and Connecticut come to mind, have passed laws adding certified behavior analysts as approved professionals to work within public schools. This allows the principal, if he or she deems a behavior analyst necessary on staff, to hire a behavior analyst as a behavior analyst rather than trying to fit that person into another job designation. We are seeing a number of interesting models where there are people who are formally trained and credentialed in behavior analysis directly working in schools, but there are numerous structural and coordination-related barriers that result in fairly slow growth of these models" (James Carr, personal communication, June 30, 2015).

While most states have little in the way of thoughtful approaches to integrating BCBAs into public education, much less have model programs, there are a handful of noteworthy examples. Here are three.

VERMONT: GETTING EVERYONE AROUND THE TABLE

Erin Maguire is the Executive Director of Student Support Services for the Chittenden Central Supervisory Union, which serves the Essex Junction, Essex Union #46, and Westford schools just east of Burlington, Vermont. "I'm in the business of ensuring that children get what they need," Maguire noted. "While diagnostic criteria may help me understand the research base applicable to their needs, I always look at students as individuals. Whether they are identified as being on the autism spectrum or not, I look at the student and what that student needs."

The breadth of the autism spectrum is detailed in the *Diagnostic and Statistical Manual of Mental Disorders* (DSM-5). It is a reality that Maguire must accept. "Whether or not a student has autism, that is only the first part of whether a child is eligible for services. The severity of the symptomology of any disability is my focus and how it impacts access to education. Whether or not the category of autism is too broad or too tight is a function of society's need to label people."

But the reasons for the increase in students on the spectrum piques Maguire's curiosity. "I think it's important not to focus only on the increase in autism, but what special education categories have decreased at the same time. Data shows a decrease in intellectual disabilities and an increase in autism in Vermont. That speaks to one end of the spectrum. There seems to be a leveling off of students identified with attention deficit and speech-language disabilities and with learning disabilities associated with the other end of the spectrum. And there are probably kids who would not have been identified with ADHD, speech-language, learning disability, or intellectual disability who are now eligible under the category of autism. Students who might have been considered in an antisocial framework are now being diagnosed as disabled. I do worry about the fidelity of diagnoses. I worry about labeling kids with data sets that I think are quite insufficient."

With medical insurance distancing itself from autism to the point that advocates organized to pass legislation in dozens of states mandating insurance coverage, public schools were left for years as the front line of treatment for children on the spectrum. In Maguire's view, "It took a while for autism to be treated anywhere other than education. Other significant disabilities were already covered under the medical framework. I don't know what caused the lack of medical attention, but it was a bad decision from a policy perspective and invited the political charge that came forward. Occupational therapy, physical therapy, and a variety of services that are important for kids on the spectrum were covered for kids with CP and for kids with other diagnoses, but for some reason autism was held off.

"There has been a lot of conversation among special education administrators about the dynamic of a new body of services for students experiencing autism spectrum disorder," noted Maguire. "We are grateful that the medical ban on services for kids with ASD is being confronted and reduced. We see this as an opportunity for collaboration across multiple agencies.

"A year ago we pulled all providers—both those providing insurance services and those providing school-based services for students on the spectrum—together to collaborate. We also included parents. We focused on a crosswalk of treatment plans to make sure we maximized the services available for students to make the greatest amount of growth. We also wanted to make sure we were not cross-treating a child because there needs to be a consistency of approach to help students generalize. If we have people providing therapy across agencies and we never talk to one another, we could actually reduce the rate of a student's progress."

Maguire continued, "This effort to coordinate services is modeled after Vermont ACT 264 that calls for a coordinated service plan. Since the autism law is pretty new, the number of services available under the insurance framework is fairly limited in Vermont. As we grow more insurance services, we will make more and more connections with our peers providing the insurance services to make sure that we do what is best for the kids.

"We are in the business to maximize growth for kids," noted Maguire. "FAPE doesn't require that. FAPE requires that we provide educational benefit for students. I can say with surety that we regularly work beyond that. Classroom teachers want the best outcomes for their students. Legally there is a floor of benefit, but emotionally, socially, and culturally, teachers want students to reach their potential, and we try to find ways to do that. Insurance services are now one of the opportunities we have to help kids reach their potential and they are new to our system."

Maguire continued, "Education has built a robust array of services for students on the spectrum and now we have added access to insurance services. Insurance cannot supplant the services already built into education, but in adding them together you can catapult the service delivery system for students on the autism spectrum into a greater level of care. This rings true for any state where autism was limited to education. Education built a service continuum that was expected to stay intact, and then on top of it came the insurance services."

Maguire recognizes the differences for a child receiving ABA in a clinic setting versus in a classroom. "A divide sometimes takes place between the very rigid approach that a strict ABA framework holds and the challenges associated with generalizing skills from that approach in a classroom. In a treatment setting, ABA application is pure. In a public school setting with inclusion expected, ABA becomes somewhat diluted and challenging. We have not gone far enough with the true integration of BCBAs and ABA inside of public education. Yet, I have had students in strict ABA programs that actually limit their participation with their peers and their opportunities for generalization.

"We often think of ABA as a package," noted Maguire. "I would like to see the integration of an ABA framework within the context of a public school. We're not there yet, but we're on the precipice of that conversation. It's important that researchers and experts in this field start thinking about that issue in ways that break boundaries. I have more and more people with whom I work wanting to become BCBAs. There's such a growing need for them. There's recognition of the incredible value of ABA" (Erin Maguire, personal communication, September 11, 2015).

IOWA: A BCBA IN THE DEPARTMENT OF EDUCATION

In 2009, Sean Casey and his wife, both BCBAs, were living in Pennsylvania. He was a professor at Penn State engaged in research in feeding disorders, and she worked for the New Jersey Department of Education. When family circumstances called Sean's wife back home to Iowa, she found a similar position in the Iowa Department of Education to the one she held in New Jersey. She also found an open position in the department for a challenging behavior consultant and encouraged Sean to apply. During his interview, the committee head went off script and asked Sean how he would fix the behavioral issues in Iowa. Sean replied, "If Iowa is anything like Pennsylvania, I would stop the false positives from doing Functional Behavioral Assessments (FBAs) as they are likely making behavior worse!" He recalled, "The next question from the committee head was, 'When can you start?'"

When Casey arrived in Iowa, the state's public schools, like those across the country, were reeling from the financial crisis. "There was a bit of luck involved. The stimulus dollars from the Obama Administration were perfectly suited for a project to improve behavioral services in Iowa. We went to our nine area education agencies, and 43 people volunteered to begin a training program to properly address challenging behaviors. Of those 43 people, only six reported having any significant knowledge of FBAs. So we embarked on a process to improve services. Six years later, it is still going on. We are now into our second and third generation of training. A lot of these members work on autism teams as well as challenging behavior teams for kids who do not have autism."

As a BCBA, Casey is data driven and knows that data is not only needed to measure results, but that it is also the key to ongoing funding, especially when his projects improve services for children while saving money. His focus is on the 8,500 students with behavioral concerns in their IEP. "Right now we have 33 full-time equivalents, a total of 54 people statewide who we are working with. We grade them based on the National Institutes of Health rubric of expert, advanced-level, or emerging skill. When we started, none of our people even had a 50 percent knowledge base in this area. Now we have people that are advanced-level in their skills, and we are expanding this project. Eventually, the state will need 127 people statewide focused on improving challenging student behavior."

Casey continued, "It's not a train-the-trainer model. We don't do a two-day workshop and then send these people off to train others. This is a process that we've gone through, and we're still working on the refinements. Our data indicates that it takes about two years for us to train a person skilled in this particular domain. That two-year time frame has a lot to do with the reality of training everybody in the state at the same time. If we were able to do this intensely with smaller groups of people, it may be faster, but it may not be any faster as well; we simply do not know. We're working with people from Sioux City all the way over to Keokuk—the two opposite corners of the state—and everywhere in between this relatively rural state.

"In some regards, it is BCBA-light," noted Casey. "BCBA is a credential in our field that broadly spans several domains within the field of behavior analysis, and this credential has its own advantages and disadvantages. For example, we have some BCBAs in our state who work in autism programs that don't know anything about how to address challenging behavior. They could provide a good Lovaas-type of program, but outside of that, they don't have the skills to address challenging student behavior and vice versa. The individuals that we're working with do not receive training in a Lovaas-type model or social skills training, or in feeding or communication issues. Nonetheless, every single one of our people who went on to become a BCBA passed the examination the first time around (the first-time pass rate is about 54 percent nationwide).

"One of the biggest measures we have to date is that we reduced out-of-district placement referrals from 5.3 percent to 1.7 percent in a matter of four years within our active regions. If we scaled that to the entire state, we would save $12.5 million in Iowa on that one measure alone," explained Casey. "I don't want to be doing something just because it was on *Oprah*. I want to be doing something because there is a solid research base behind it and we have been effective implementing it. My work at the department is evidence-based and is actually impacting positive change in our state and saving money" (Sean Casey, personal communication, July 16, 2015).

INDIANA: TWO PEOPLE COORDINATING COLLECTIVE IMPACT

Cathy Pratt and Stephan Viehweg have trained more than 103,000 people during the last three years on evidence-based practices. Pratt is a former teacher, a BCBA, and a director at the Indiana Resource Center for Autism. Viehweg is a clinical social worker and a professor at the Indiana University School of Medicine. Their mission is to pull people together and foster communication between professionals for the benefit of children with disabilities.

Pratt said, "My office is located at Indiana University in Bloomington. We are a statewide training and technical assistance program, and we work very closely with school districts all over the state of Indiana. We have autism leaders in all of our special education planning districts and have trained more than 400 teams statewide. We coach on implementing evidence-based practices."

Viehweg is a faculty member of Indiana's Leadership Education in Neurodevelopmental and Related Disabilities (LEND) interdisciplinary training program. LEND programs provide long-term, graduate-level interdisciplinary training as well as interdisciplinary services and care. The purpose of the LEND training program is to improve the health of infants, children, and adolescents with disabilities. He noted, "We help individuals without early identification or early intervention be better prepared for entering special education; we also help with the transition from early intervention to special education. We help make sure that they understand what the constraints are, what services are available, and how they can access those services and get them paid for."

Viehweg continued, "Cathy and I are committed to modeling collaboration and sharing to accomplish greater things. We have more than enough evidence to show that we are more successful as a state when we collaborate and are committed to letting our smartest people work together to find solutions. We strive for communication and conversation about the challenges that professionals and families with children with disabilities face. When we pulled an ABA workgroup together, we included related professionals with diverse backgrounds and experience. We developed a work plan for this group, and we get together every three months to develop the materials and to stay connected."

Pratt noted, "When we discuss current issues, we have ground rules about how we proceed and stay connected on topics to make sure that we don't undermine each other's efforts. This takes work. I am continually checking in with people and sharing information, and Steve is exceptional at that as well. For me, it has been a really good learning experience of getting people to sit down at the table and realize that we all want the same thing, we all want good things for families and children."

Viehweg continued, "If we think about the end game, it influences what we do now in early intervention." Pratt added, "We saw there was a need in

Indiana, and we made a commitment to put our resources toward bringing people together (Cathy Pratt and Stephan Viehweg, personal communications, August 4 and 7, 2015).

BACK TO REALITY

Sherzod Abdukadirov, a researcher on government regulation, noted, "There are very few industries as regulated as education. There is no other industry where you would be tied to a particular provider. Having a single regulation apply across so many different types of schools is definitely a problem. The biggest weakness of regulation is that the law applies equally to everybody." While that may sound very appealing, very egalitarian, Abdukadirov emphasized that such an approach results in measuring what schools do rather than what they accomplish. "It leads to putting a check mark on an IEP. Whether that activity actually leads to any improvement is still questionable. It is a lot easier to track, but it basically precludes teachers from trying other things that may be better" (Sherzod Abdukadirov, personal communication, July 13, 2015).

Abdukadirov's scholarship on education regulation pulls one back to earth after a glimpse of hope and sanity offered in three programs across the country. But the reality is that McGuire, Casey, Pratt, and Viehweg are exceptions—excellent exceptions—but nonetheless exceptions as professionals in the public sphere who are active at the crossroads of autism and behavior analysis. It is not a stretch to imagine that most public school leaders, when asked about behavior analysis, would respond like Jeb Bush did to Aubrey Daniels. The pending reauthorization of IDEA provides a national stage on which parents, policy experts, special educators, and advocates will debate how to improve the law with all implications laid bare in a manner that no education leaders will be able to ignore.

REFERENCES

Behavior Analyst Certification Board. 2016, August 9. "Certificant Registry." Retrieved from http://info.bacb.com/o.php?page=100155.

Centers for Disease Control and Prevention. 2015. "Autism Spectrum Disorder (ASD): Screening and Diagnosis" (Last Updated: February 2015). Retrieved from http://www.cdc.gov/ncbddd/autism/screening.html (July 27, 2016).

Mandell, D. S., Morales, K. H., Xie, M., Polsky, D., Stahmer, A., and Marcus, S. C. 2010. "County-Level Variation in the Prevalence of Medicaid-Enrolled Children with Autism Spectrum Disorders." *Journal of Autism and Developmental Disorders* 40(10): 1241–46.

Chapter Nine

Suggestions for Reauthorization: Unbundling IDEA

Let's forget the separate categories of general education and special education and just have education for all children and all the appropriate supports and services and technology needed.

—Margaret Masimore

State fights matter, frankly, even more than federal fights do right now because actual movements happen on the state level.

—Joe Fuld

Reauthorization of the Individuals with Disabilities Education Act should take place before the year 2020. What might the atmosphere be for that process? Former Autism Speaks attorney Daniel Unumb expects that "school districts are going to be loaded for bear, knowing that the expectations of disability groups are going to be far higher for a number of reasons. One thing that could make the process less contentious would be for Congress to step up and do the right thing and say, 'Yes, we understand our obligations and need to do this. We need to step up and start providing the real federal funding that was always intended by IDEA, so that we are not just sticking the states with this obligation.' That would benefit everybody in the long run. That could go a long way to mitigating the scorched earth policy of the states" (Daniel Unumb, personal communication, July 18, 2016).

Political science professor John Pitney is brief in his expectation for the mood during reauthorization, "It is going to be like a university faculty meeting on PCP" (John Pitney, personal communication, July 13, 2016). University faculty meetings can be notoriously uncivil.

Whether the reauthorization process proves to be civil or cantankerous, will our nation's collective values and scientific developments be reflected in the next iteration of the law? Will we take what we learned during 40 years of implementation in special education into account? Systemic improvements, reductions, creative solutions, and imagining the unthinkable provide four organizational rubrics for thoughts offered by the voices heard in this book. The book ends by framing the conflicts within special education and within the world of ABA and examines the economic treatment of autism, concluding with a call for a new approach in serving students with exceptionalities, especially those with autism.

SYSTEMIC IMPROVEMENTS

As a member of the Council of Administrators of Special Education, a legislative and policy committee, Vermont's Erin Maguire is connected to federal special education policy. "The work we do in CASE comes directly from the field. One of our main focus points is mental health—specifically, the impact of experiencing autism spectrum disorder and the impact on the family managing with severe ASD. We have deep concern about the lack of community-based services for people experiencing mental health challenges, and that would certainly include kids with autism spectrum disorder."

Maguire continued, "The changes we need at the federal level are specific to two things. One is to ensure that students have a high quality educational experience and that they are not marginalized or excluded based on disability. And the second is that we have the flexibility to design programs that address the needs of kids, that we are not constrained by federal rules and labels" (Erin Maguire, personal communication, September 11, 2015).

"At least in California," noted California's Maureen O'Leary Burness, "I do not see autism being separated from special education as a medical issue. I believe fully that schools are going to continue to be partners, and that we're still going to have an IEP. If IDEA changes everything, everyone will need to respond to that, but I do not see it as an either-or thing—either medical or special education—even for families with great means. The school districts are still a resource to them, and I do not think they're going to give that up" (Maureen O'Leary Burness, personal communication, August 5, 2015).

In April 2016, the American Association of School Administrators (AASA) issued *Rethinking Special Education Due Process: A Proposal for the Next Reauthorization of the Individuals with Disabilities Education Act.* "The report contends modifications to the current due process system could greatly reduce, if not eliminate, the burdensome and often costly litigation that does not necessarily ensure measureable educational gains for special education students" (Pudelski 2016, 2).

The report noted the cost associated with due process: "The average legal fees for a district involved in a due process hearing were $10,512.50. Districts compelled to compensate parents for their attorney's fees averaged $19,241.38. The expenditures associated with the verdict of the due process hearing averaged districts $15,924.14. For districts that chose to settle with a parent prior to the adjudication of the due process hearing, the settlement costs averaged $23,827.34" (Pudelski 2016, 3). A footnote, however, explains that the Council of School Attorneys maintains much higher average cost estimates overall. AASA's proposed changes to the due process procedure include the following points:

- Add IEP facilitation to the list of options a district can use to resolve disputes with parents by authorizing districts to contract with a state-approved, trained IEP facilitator. Because most conflict centers on the creation of the IEP, a neutral, state-provided, trained facilitator could help parties reach agreement before any legal paperwork is filed. There is considerable evidence documenting the effectiveness of IEP facilitation in resolving disputes between parents and districts.
- If facilitation fails, the district and parents would jointly select an independent, neutral special education consultant designated by the state to review evidence of the child's disability and advise the parties on how to devise a suitable compromise IEP. The consultant would have 21 days to access student evaluations; interview parents and school personnel; observe the student in school; examine the school's services; and review the student's academic performance. The consultant would then write a report recommending an IEP for the student. The district and parent would be obligated to follow the consultant-designed IEP for a mutually agreed upon period of time.
- If either party were dissatisfied with the consultant IEP after attempting to test it, that party could file a lawsuit, and the consultant's notes and model IEP would be included as part of the record in any litigation.
- Mediation remains an option available to both parties for resolving IDEA disputes prior to litigation; however, mediation would occur after the IEP consultancy process failed. The only individuals required to attend the me-

diation would be the trained mediator, the parents, and two district representatives.

- If the parent wished to pursue compensatory education or reimbursement for expenses associated with obtaining private education in the absence of the school district's provision of Free Appropriate Public Education (FAPE), the parent could do so in court only after having attempted to find agreement with the district through the facilitation and consultancy model. (Pudelski 2016, 4)

Special education attorney Sonja Kerr objects to AASA's proposal to change due process and feels that dedication to training will greatly reduce litigation. "I don't think the solution, as the American Association of School Administrators has proposed, is to eliminate or reduce parental access to special education due process hearings. I think the solution needs to be much bigger than that, and I think it would basically have two elements. One element would be that school districts would be required to train their staff in several problematic aspects that would affect the majority of children. Those would include applied behavior analysis, assistive technology, the Orton-Gillingham reading approach, and so on. The second element would involve transition services and counseling services. If we actually had staff at every school, or a reasonable number within every district, who could provide those services, we would see a lot less litigation" (Sonja Kerr, personal communication, December 16, 2015).

"In the reauthorization of IDEA, a critical component has to be higher education and the preparation given to general educators," noted Janna Lilly, government relations director for the Texas Council of Administrators of Special Education. "We are asking our general education teachers to provide universal design for learning, but a general education teacher in a preservice university program gets one class on exceptionalities, and that class is generally a week on autism, a week on emotional disturbance, a week on intellectual disability, and so forth. Then we throw those teachers into a classroom, and they may only have five students in their entire class that are what we would call typically developing general education children who do not need accommodations. Among the others, they may need English as a Second Language programs, they may need gifted and talented accommodations, or they may need special education or 504 services. So higher education needs to step up to the plate and redesign its programs to prepare general educators to serve all kinds of students."

Lilly also encouraged a repositioning of response to intervention (RTI). "Response to intervention is currently situated within IDEA. It is a general education model, and I would love to see it totally out of IDEA and just in ESEA (now ESSA). Parents ultimately don't care where their children get the needed service, but parents know our general education box isn't big enough to give some kids the specificity that they need" (Janna Lilly, personal communication, August 12, 2015).

Special programs director Phyllis Wolfram noted, "The U.S. Department of Education has come out with a new term, results-driven accountability (RDA), to put the focus more on outcomes for students versus the compliance pieces. So, in the state of Missouri, our administrators group has taken on that charge, and we are investing quite a bit of time in unifying general and special education. We don't want to look at reinventing special education in and of itself, and Missouri isn't alone; colleagues across the United States are doing the same thing.

"I think that there will be some significant changes in the reauthorization if the people who are currently working in special education step up and voice what they believe needs to happen and if the legislators listen," Wolfram continued. "Right now, we are implementing and being governed by a law that hasn't changed significantly in the last two reauthorizations, except to become much more regulatory" (Phyllis Wolfram, personal communication, July 22, 2015).

REDUCTIONS

"As a special education policy, there are a lot of people who believe that the percentage of children and youth with disabilities should more properly be 3 percent," noted Vanderbilt's Douglas Fuchs. "While I don't support this, I think there is going to be a concerted effort to try to write certain disabilities out of the law, and to do it not necessarily in one fell swoop, but to begin a process by which learning disabilities are no longer seen as disabilities.

Fuchs added, "I think it is a way of dramatically downsizing special education, of dramatically reducing the number of kids with disabilities in the special education enterprise. I think implicit is a very negative view of special education and, interestingly, a wildly optimistic view of general education. And in my view, special education doesn't deserve such pessimism and general education doesn't deserve such optimism" (Douglas Fuchs, personal communication, July 16, 2015).

Director of special education preschool services Brenda Van Gorder offered, "In the next reauthorization, it would not surprise me if they redefine
learning disabilities. I do not think the category will go away, but I think that
they will redefine it" (Brenda Van Gorder, personal communication, October
9, 2015).

Missouri's Phyllis Wolfram said, "We need a paradigm shift to where
we're really looking at special education as meeting the needs of those students who are truly disabled. If we implement a multitiered system of support, we will be more intentional and data driven when identifying students
with disabilities. The majority of our special education students are now
spending the majority of their time in a general education classroom. Currently, some of those students' needs are being met and some are not, because we're not implementing a truly intentional structure for meeting their
needs. If we implemented a true multitiered system of support, teachers
would have a strong framework for meeting the needs of all learners" (Phyllis Wolfram, personal communication, July 22, 2015).

Patricia Latham is a past president of the Learning Disabilities Association of America. She is also an attorney and the author of a number of books
on special education law. Latham does not think learning disabilities are at
risk in IDEA's next reauthorization. "That would be, of course, a very big
mistake because specific learning disability is a term recognized under IDEA
and in many court decisions, and specific learning disorder is recognized in
the DSM-5. The typical situation is that a person is diagnosed as having a
specific learning disability after receiving a battery of testing administered by
a psychologist or other type of specialist. It is very real, very concrete. You
can measure how the individual's performance is impacted in particular areas. So it would be difficult for me to imagine simply eliminating something
that currently is a listed disability under IDEA and recognized as an impairment under ADA."

Latham continued, "Some people may have very mild issues. And I think
it's generally recognized that where the issues are very mild, needs are sometimes met without a great deal of intervention. But, for many other students,
where the learning issues are much more significant and are disabilities under
IDEA, special education and related services are required to address those
particular disabilities. So, I cannot imagine that the term learning disability
would simply be deleted from IDEA" (Patricia Latham, personal communication, March 10, 2016).

Regulatory scholar Patrick McLaughlin might side with Latham, "Whenever a regulatory program is created, it is really difficult to get rid of it because of the special interest groups that will then try to protect it. Special interests are ultimately going to play a large role in any sort of democratic process in the United States" (Patrick McLaughlin, personal communication, August 7, 2105).

CREATIVE SOLUTIONS

Wolfram offered, "When we look at children with autism, other health impairments, or those children with emotional disturbance who have significant needs, we need to create more alternative options for providing services. Twenty years ago we did not have that many alternative schools, but there's a good group of students with significant mental health needs that we need to look at differently, and it can't just be special education doing something different. It needs to be a collaborative effort with education and community resources working together to meet the needs of those children. There are so many environmental factors that play a role with those students; it takes more to educate them. It is not necessarily unbundling all of IDEA, but it might be clarifying and restructuring pieces of IDEA in order to serve these students better" (Phyllis Wolfram, personal communication, July 22, 2015).

Superintendent Patricia Fagan Greco hopes that reauthorization will simplify the ability of various professionals to work together for the benefit of the child. "There are a couple of things that I think we have to figure out in meeting the needs of children. The privacy laws themselves create a barrier. On the one hand, privacy laws are a direct benefit to individuals and the rights of individuals. On the other hand, when you're looking at the ability to pull together professionals across organizations in order to figure out how to intervene, who has what skill sets, and what the collective capacity is around a shared purpose of supporting children and families, it can become impossible. So one area that we have to figure out is, how do we more effectively bridge across agencies with shared purpose in order to intervene around student needs?"

Fagan Greco added, "I think the ability to actually interact with other agencies regarding a really involved student should remain all the way through that student's education career so that those partnerships are available when needed. I think that partnership and the ability to work with therapists between the clinical side and the educational side can be value-added" (Patricia Fagan Greco, personal communication, July 23, 2015).

"Let's front-load the system to help children achieve and get them to a level of self-sufficiency so that they do not need adult services," opined policy specialist Greg Boris. "What I'm suggesting is to front-load the front-loaded system with not just quality pre-K but with quality birth-to-3 access as well as good prenatal care and good preconception information" (Greg Boris, personal communication, June 15, 2015).

Randy Lewis, now retired, was an executive in supply chain and logistics at Walgreens. He created a program at the company's many distribution centers across the country that resulted in employing more than 1,000 people with disabilities who earn the same pay, perform the same jobs, and are held to the same performance standards as other employees. He is a noted advocate for employing those with disabilities and pushes for services at the other end of "childhood." Lewis believes that IEPs should be extended to age 25 for those whose disabilities create significant barriers to employment and that school systems should be measured not only by the number of graduates who pursue postsecondary education but also by the "percent of individuals who had an IEP and are employed at age 25."

To increase employment opportunities, Lewis proposes a community-wide partnership that engages parents, schools, local businesses, and local government to create summer internships beginning at age 16 and continuing through the end of transition. "Local government could provide program administration, schools the educational support, and businesses the internship opportunities. Beginning in high school, academics could include time allotted for teaching executive, problem-solving, and advocacy skills that improve likelihood of success in the workplace. Job coaches to support those in internships could be recruited from the local community; returning college students, for example, could provide on-the-job support for interns."

Lewis continued, "By the time they have completed transition, each will have a complete resume of experience and a complete coaching file including the type of jobs and motivation and all the other things that an employer would need to know. If we were to take the view that our job as a community is to best prepare *all* our children for adulthood, we would unleash the imagination of the local community, save a lot of money, and have a better world" (Randy Lewis, personal communication, July 11, 2016).

Daniel Unumb also sees the value in extending services for those who need support for employability. "There is a huge issue about transitioning to adult life. What is the school's responsibility? It has responsibilities under the IDEA, but in too many cases, it is just a planning exercise that is carried out imperfectly even on that limited ground. We do have the capability to integrate the vocational system with the school system to actually give the kind of instruction and support that would allow students to become employed. We can do internships and have concrete, hands-on experience that will result in that child being employed at 25. And yes, that may require a greater dedication of resources, but it's going to have a tremendous payoff" (Daniel Unumb, personal communication, July 18, 2016).

IMAGINING THE UNTHINKABLE

Perhaps it is the freedom that retirement allows, but former Nashville special education director Margaret Masimore noted, "If you ask me, they just need to start over. Let's forget the separate categories of general education and special education and just have education for all children and all the appropriate supports and services and technology needed.

"What we have today is what I crudely call pieces parts. We are educating students in pieces, in parts—I have the language, you have the motor, and you get the classroom stuff. Nobody is working together to integrate all of it into an appropriate program that wraps around and supports the student so the student can learn and function and grow up to be a contributing member of society. I think most special education students can be contributing members, but the way that they are being taught today is not doing the job.

"Lawsuits and the evolution of the law have compounded the problem as opposed to improving it," noted Masimore. "For years we were evaluated and monitored on whether or not we had every box filled out just right, but nobody ever looked at the content of what was happening for the student. The process didn't and doesn't care a bit about the outcome for the student" (Margaret Masimore, personal communication, June 17, 2015).

In 1978, the U.S. Supreme Court ruled in *Regents of the University of California v. Bakke* that affirmative action is permissible under the Civil Rights Act of 1964. Since *Bakke*, there have been numerous legal challenges to affirmative action policies, particularly in higher education admissions procedures. Supporters of affirmative action find the policies helpful in creating a more diverse student body or a more diverse workplace and in providing those groups, which have long suffered discrimination, an improved chance at advancement. Challengers argue that affirmative action creates reverse discrimination, that attitudes and practices have evolved since the Civil Rights Act, and that affirmative action measures are therefore no longer needed.

Public Law 94-142, the Education for All Handicapped Children Act, was passed in 1975 in order to improve the education of some 2 million children who were poorly served in public schools and to guarantee admission to more than 1 million children who had been denied access to public education. More than 40 years have passed since its passage. Have the values of Public Law 94-142 and IDEA taken root? Could the argument that is made by opponents of affirmative action be also made of IDEA? Have federal and state governments successfully inculcated measures to guarantee access and a free appropriate public education for all children with handicapping conditions? What would happen if IDEA were not reauthorized? What would happen if under an ESSA-mentality more authority was granted to the states regarding special education matters and if the states then dispersed that authority to local districts?

Is Margaret Masimore's "forget the separate categories of general education and special education and just have education for all children and all the appropriate supports and services and technology needed" a vision whose time has come? While there is no move to repeal IDEA on the horizon, considering such a prospect provides an opportunity to consider how a school district would respond. Without the power of the law, would there be a commitment to keep in place the processes, guarantees, and values of IDEA? Would the schoolhouse doors remain open for all children? Would children with special needs continue to receive a larger portion of the budget than their representative numbers? Would a director of special education maintain a seat on the superintendent's cabinet? Has IDEA done its job or is it still needed to guarantee access and FAPE and to keep the bad old days at bay? Does the question even matter?

It matters because answering yes or no sets into motion a realization of the complex organizational and social realities that our nation's dedication to special education has created. If one says, "Yes, IDEA has done its job and can be eliminated," a vision of protective walls of the law and the processes and the specializations coming down creates a nightmare reality for the students and families that are currently sheltered by those walls and for the hundreds of thousands of people whose professions are tied to current special education structures.

If one says, "No, IDEA should be adjusted as needed, but not eliminated," there is an admission that special education is not deeply rooted as a value within public education. It suggests that it is only the force of the law that bludgeons public education into fully serving students with disabilities.

The hypothetical question of eliminating IDEA matters because just 40 years ago children with handicapping conditions who should have been in school were excluded from school and because millions who attended received inferior treatment. It took a federal law to not only right a wrong but also to define that wrong, to declare that exclusion from school due to a handicapping condition was illegal. In the ensuing period, the education of children with handicapping conditions has become an established part of public education. In fact, special education, at $100 billion, is the largest portion of the $630 billion public education budget. The money is woven into the system, but not everyone embraces special education or individuals with disabilities in their hearts.

South Dakota special education leader Michelle Powers noted, "Some people will always do the right thing, but not everyone will, and that is why there are laws and why we need to enforce those laws. This is true about everything in our world, whether it's drugs, speeding, or following IDEA. Some people will always do it right, and some people won't. That is what the laws are for" (Michelle Powers, personal communication, June 10, 2016).

While Daniel Unumb noted, "I just don't believe that we are in a place to even think about an argument that we no longer need IDEA" (Daniel Unumb, personal communication, July 18, 2016), his wife, Lorri Unumb, opined that IDEA is such a poor law that its elimination may make very little difference. "So much of the law was structured to remedy a kind of blatant discrimination, and we are in a completely different place today. I don't think that I'm simply being a Pollyanna. I believe that our society and our culture have changed and that we would not tolerate that kind of discrimination against children with disabilities even without a federal law.

"I am speaking purely from the autism perspective here and not from the perspective of other disabilities, but I think IDEA is so ill-suited to provide the modifications and accommodations and the instruction that many children with autism need. Some wonder if we would be any worse off without IDEA; it is such a patchwork from state to state. It may be that removing IDEA in states where special education works better, like New York or Massachusetts, would be a disastrous step, but in states where special education doesn't work well, I wonder how much difference it would make" (Lorri Unumb, personal communication, July 18, 2016).

As Randy Lewis noted, "The ultimate aim of justice is reconciliation. Without it, there can be no lasting justice. That is, there needs to be a mandate in place until it becomes a cultural value, a reconciliation" (Randy Lewis, personal communication, July 11, 2016).

THE OPPORTUNITY OF REAUTHORIZATION

This book is about public school special education, the Individuals with Disabilities Education Act, and the growth of the behavior analysis profession and about how they relate to children with autism. The unintended consequences of laws and regulations and their failure to keep up with medical, technological, environmental, and societal developments are real. IDEA is out of touch with developments, research, and organizational structures related to autism.

The history of the United States is filled with improvements, changes, corrections, rectifications, and efforts to right wrongs. IDEA is one such example. Unfortunately, and for any number of reasons, some laws eventually become an encumbrance to the very people or idea they were meant to support or result in unintended consequences that interfere with its original purpose. While the unintended consequences of laws are legion, the number of laws that have not kept pace with medical, technological, environmental, and societal development is far greater.

Examples of regulations that fail to keep up with technological and societal changes include those related to peer-to-peer marketplaces. Companies like Airbnb, Uber, Lyft, Lending Club, and Prosper are far ahead of regulation, rather than in violation of regulation, and so fully engaged in the sharing economy that their existence, success, and future are bound to reshape the parameters of their respective industries. So what do these interesting and regulatory disruptive businesses have to do with IDEA and autism?

First, companies like Airbnb and Uber demonstrate just how quickly things are changing in the economy. Second, they illustrate how technological and scientific advancements move society. Society follows the pace of innovation, not the constraint of regulation. When the predecessor of IDEA, Public Law 94-142, was signed into law by President Ford in 1975, our world and this nation moved more slowly; there was no internet, no social media, no texting, and autism was believed to affect 1 in every 5,000 children.

Public Law 94-142 guaranteed access to a free and appropriate public education for all children regardless of handicapping conditions. Even though many public school districts had long-standing policies of education for and inclusion of children with disabilities, Public Law 94-142 protected all public school children and, as laws do, was designed to change the behavior of school districts that excluded children. Furthermore, Public Law 94-142 was designed to empower parents of children with disabilities, giving them specific rights regarding the education of their children, rights that are very different than those that govern the education of their neurotypical peers.

Current laws and practices are increasingly disconnected from the rise in the number of children identified with autism, developments in the treatment of autism, and the professionalization of the applied behavior analysis field. The focal point of this disconnection is public education, and the disconnections that surround autism and public schooling will be the most influential backdrop in the reauthorization of IDEA. But public education will be an observer rather than a participant in many of the conflicts that will shape the future.

Among those conflicts, there is significant disharmony within the field of applied behavior analysis. ABA is not a single practice but a term that encompasses a variety of approaches in using behavior analysis. Verbal behavior, discrete trial training, antecedent-based intervention, and pivotal response treatment are specific approaches that are among dozens of evidence-based interventions that fly under the flag of ABA. Having an array of approaches under one banner is not necessarily bad. Speech therapists also have dozens of approaches in their discipline, as do psychiatrists, oncologists, and many other fields.

The immediate challenge for ABA is one of self-regulation and self-definition as it fights for a place at the table within public education and for recognition of its therapeutic and economic value in terms of insurance, Medicaid, and private funding. The discipline needs to codify what it is, what it stands for, and what is acceptable and what is not. It has a significant organizational and academic battle ahead.

The profession of applied behavior analysis will need to befriend other disciplines. ABA's professional rivals will accept it less grudgingly as it defines itself, establishes firmer borders, and as its purpose and approach are better known and utilized. ABA has a lot to offer, not only in terms of behavioral health, but also in terms of organizational management, sustainability efforts, forensics, diplomacy, et cetera. But any science with such wide and varied applicability can easily lose its identity and its way.

Applied behavior analysis will also need to prove its case with health insurers. Since 2007, more than 40 states have passed legislation mandating coverage for autism, and some identify ABA as a preferred treatment. Health insurance companies want to know what they are paying for as well as basic information like the probable length of treatment and expected outcome.

Medical services use Current Procedural Terminology (CPT) codes established by the American Medical Association to report procedures and services for reimbursement by public and private health insurance providers. Category I codes cover well-established, widely delivered, FDA-approved practices and procedures. Category III codes cover procedures or services for which, among other requirements, actual or potential clinical efficacy is supported in peer-reviewed literature.

Applied behavior analysis rests in Category III, which is much less stable and predictable than Category I. Category III codes are temporary, still awaiting clinical evidence of efficacy, and rates are set by payer sources and can be changed up to two times a year. It may take years for ABA to earn the stability of Category I CPT coding, but workgroups are already in place to help make it happen, gathering the required input from other professions and managing the incoming data in order to meet the rigorous standards of Category I.

The first major insurer to recognize ABA was TRICARE, the insurer of the U.S. Armed Forces. With so many families in the military, TRICARE created a demonstration project in 2008 to make ABA accessible for young children. The demonstration project is set to undergo review in 2017 and 2018 so that TRICARE can better understand what it purchased and what the impact has been on children who received ABA services. This is the first major external review that the field of ABA must navigate. In its response to TRICARE, the discipline of ABA may begin to define its borders, treatments, and protocols. The process will have both winners and losers within the discipline, but it will be a much-needed step in the profession's advancement.

But public education does not have to be an observer when it comes to ABA and special education. Applied behavior analysis is a tool that every school and every school district should include. While inter- and intraprofessional battles transpire and ABA wrestles with insurance reimbursement and CPT codes, the value ABA offers to children with autism and to a wide range of DSM-5 disabilities as well as the value it offers to neurotypical children is real and measurable.

State departments of education can recognize BCBAs as certified professionals that are needed within schools. School districts and teacher associations can create the appropriate recognition for the profession in contracts and assign terms and conditions in keeping with the purview of the position and with the value it can bring at either a school or district level.

As insurance brings new resources to the benefit of children with autism, schools can take a tip from Vermont's Erin Maguire and Wisconsin's Patricia Fagan Greco and invite health care providers into the dialog for the benefit of the child. Schools can create the very best programs for children with autism, competing with other schools as aggressively as they do in interscholastic sports. Rather than fear the results of having an oversubscribed exemplary program for children with autism, schools can focus on the benefits that a state-of-the-art autism program will bring the community—more residents, more skilled workers, more property taxes, healthier families, and a more inclusive community.

The discussion just ahead about the reauthorization of IDEA provides an opportunity for schools, states, parents, and advocacy groups to voice their vision of a better future for children with autism and for all children. With so much focus on autism, it is potentially the pivot point for many changes in IDEA. Will autism receive unique treatment in the reauthorization? If autism gets special treatment, why not other handicapping conditions like emotional disturbance? Is the devil we know better than the devil we have yet to meet? Will public education fight changes in IDEA or welcome multiple paths to service for children with autism? Will the law be adjusted for different disabilities? In keeping with the speed of research, will the reauthorization time be shortened going forward?

As ESEA has evolved into ESSA, with states regaining more of their historic role in the state function of education, political consultant Joe Fuld's insights on the return to the importance of states offers a view of what might be. "Issues have moved away, especially advocacy in general, from being a federal concern to being state and local issues that people have to take on. That has happened over time and is very clear when it comes to advocacy. To really move something, you cannot just have a national presence; you need to have a local presence where people are making a difference on the state and local level, whether it's an education issue or any other issue. State fights matter, frankly, even more than federal fights do right now because actual movements happen on the state level" (Joe Fuld, personal communication, March 22, 2016).

In the reauthorization of IDEA, public education has an opportunity to recapture the high ground in special education that it seems to have lost in the rules and forced administration. Children should not have to pay for the organizational inadequacies of the education system, for the underfunding of education, or for the quest of financial gain on the part of insurers. But they do. In recent decades, special education has drifted from its role as a champion of access and of care for those with disabilities to a compliance role burdened by mandates and limited by inadequate resources.

Vanderbilt's Douglas Fuchs thinks that the lack of intensity and the lack of evidence-based effectiveness found in typical special education programs opened the door for behavior analysis. "The reason for the rise of these Board Certified Behavior Analysts is in good measure a reflection of the failure of schools—of the incapacity of schools—to provide intensity of services, and not just for kids with autism, but for all kinds of kids with all kinds of labels and even for kids without labels who are still very much at risk for school failure. There is no longer an intensity of instruction capacity at the building level" (Douglas Fuchs, personal communication, July 16, 2015).

FINAL THOUGHTS

The opening of public school doors to students with handicapping conditions was based on the same legal premise as *Brown v. Board of Education of Topeka*. The goal was access. Decades of legal battles chipped away at the myth of "separate but equal" until it finally crumbled with *Brown*. Less than two decades later, the denial of access to those with disabilities also fell away. Forty years ago access was a victory, but access without educational opportunities parallel to those without disabilities is not enough.

The many goals of public education include preparing students to care for themselves, to hold a job, to live independently, and to contribute to the wider community. The families of children with special needs have the same goals for their children and seek special education programs and services that help fulfill those goals. There is no question that it costs far more in time and money to reach those goals for a student on the severe end of the autism spectrum compared with a neurotypical student. But the laws that assure access for children with disabilities have been woefully silent on outcomes, whereas outcomes for neurotypical students have been a national fixation for several decades.

Determining outcomes for students with disabilities is by definition an individual process. Rolling up progress for students with IEPs is difficult to impossible, especially in comparison to rolling up progress for students without disabilities. Addressing the opportunities that should come with access must be a major focus in the reauthorization of IDEA. It should be a redefinition of who is covered by the law, a clarification of objectives for students under the law, and a full funding of the resources needed to meet those objectives. Reauthorization is an opportunity to change the pattern of thought and action that has become the norm, because when money matters, it really is the children who pay.

The reauthorization of IDEA is coming at an opportune time. Not only have technologies and the behavioral sciences and neurosciences, as well as the organization of advocacy groups, moved dramatically forward compared to 2004, but our society has also stepped ahead in terms of acceptance. There is an opportunity in the reauthorization to move into a post-mandate, post-tolerance era—an era in which the objective is to address the needs of the student and prepare him or her, as much as possible, for a full and independent life.

The way our society treats individuals with disabilities is a cultural paradigm; it is woven into the fabric of society. When a child is born with a developmental problem or a severe medical challenge, we have sympathy for the family. We consider it a challenge to care for a child with Down syndrome and are sad when a ramp is built to provide access to a home. We miss the opportunity to celebrate life. Our utilitarian attitude and desire for functionality blind us to the possibilities of different and hopeful outcomes.

Children with disabilities are not any less or any more than children without disabilities; they are just different. The reauthorization of IDEA gives us a chance to provide all children with what they need. This is a nation of greatness and plenty, and our children deserve to share and contribute to our collective wealth. The law can be modified to give all children the support and services they need to be the most independent and self-sustaining citizens possible.

All parents work and pray to raise children who will stand on their own feet, take care of themselves, and participate in society as contributing adults. Parents of children with disabilities want nothing less. It may take more training, it may take more time, and it may take more money to help a severely challenged young person to independence, but, for most, it is not impossible if given the appropriate supports. And the long-term cost savings of independence for society are undeniable but constantly kicked down the road.

The unbundling of IDEA means that one size does not fit all. Just as, in order to stay relevant and compete, mainstream public education has developed a multitude of choices for families, so the time has also come for such options to be available for children with disabilities. IDEA could be divided into tracks for mild, moderate, and severe disabilities. It could be expanded to age 25 under qualifying circumstances. It could establish protocols, treatments, and expectations or make an IEP portable. It could even unite FERPA and HIPAA and establish common ground for some disabilities. It could require special education to keep up with the sciences and techniques that offer the greatest hope and progress for individuals with disabilities. Without a doubt, the next reauthorization will dramatically change the nature and execution of special education.

Several years ago the disabilities community and a major hospital celebrated a joint venture. Young adults with autism were hired to sterilize hospital instruments and to wash and fold towels. The young workers were excellent at sterilizing instruments. They were also excellent at washing and folding towels. But they were not excellent at behaving in a socially appropriate manner, particularly in elevators. The program ended, not because the young workers were unable to adequately perform job tasks or contribute, but because hospital staff and patients had a culturally defined view of appropriate social behavior, a view that did not leave room for a person with autism.

Children with special needs are not a problem. The problem rests with adults who have a narrowly defined view of "normal," with those who are uncomfortable with the politics and the money involved in giving the severely challenged the supports and services they need to gain independence. Unbundling the Individuals with Disabilities Education Act means moving beyond tolerance to acceptance, beyond floors to ceilings, beyond individual battles to collective impact, and beyond the public-private dichotomy. Unbundling IDEA means moving toward a nation united to educate and serve all children to their maximum capabilities.

REFERENCES

Pudelski, S. 2016. *Rethinking Special Education Due Process: A Proposal for the Next Reauthorization of the Individuals with Disabilities Education Act.* American Association of School Administrators. Retrieved from http://www.aasa.org/uploadedFiles/Policy _and_Advocacy/Public_Policy_Resources/Special_Education/AASARethinkingSpecialEd-DueProcess.pdf.

United States Social Security Administration. 2014. *FY 2014 Budget Overview*. Retrieved from http://www.ssa.gov/budget/FY14Files/2014FJ.pdf.

Author Index

About the Authors

Mark K. Claypool is the founder and chief executive officer of ChanceLight Behavioral Health, Therapy and Education, the nation's leading provider of behavior, physical, occupational, and speech therapy and alternative and special education programs for children and young adults. In recognition of the company's social mission to offer hope, Claypool was named the EY Entrepreneur of the Year® 2016 in the social responsibility category in the Southeast.

Claypool obtained a bachelor's degree in psychology and a master of arts degree in sociology from Middle Tennessee State University. He is president of the board of directors of Book'em, a Nashville nonprofit that seeks to inspire a love of books and reading in all children, and a judge of the annual Penn Graduate School of Education Business Plan Competition. He is a frequent speaker about the value of public-private partnerships in education and behavioral health, and coauthor of *We're in This Together: Public-Private Partnerships in Special and At-Risk Education* (2015).

John M. McLaughlin, PhD, is an executive vice president and the director of research and analytics for ChanceLight Behavioral Health, Therapy and Education, formerly Educational Services of America. He has been with the company since 1999. Prior to joining ChanceLight, McLaughlin founded Benton Hall School in Nashville, now in its 40th year; was a tenured professor of educational administration at St. Cloud State University in Minnesota; and, through the 1990s, wrote monthly on education reform in *The Education Industry Report*.

McLaughlin has spoken extensively to groups ranging from the American Association of School Administrators to the World Bank. His first book of fiction, *The Last Year of the Season* (2014), was followed by a work of nonfiction, *We're in This Together: Public-Private Partnerships in Special and At-Risk Education* (2015), also coauthored with Mark K. Claypool. He holds degrees from Peabody College of Vanderbilt University, the University of Chicago, and the University of Minnesota.

CPSIA information can be obtained
at www.ICGtesting.com
Printed in the USA
BVOW08s0636150217
476213BV00002B/2/P

9 781475 834970